Fieldwork

Landscape Architecture Europe

Fieldwork

Edited by the Landscape Architecture Europe Foundation (LAE)

Birkhäuser – Publishers for Architecture
Basel · Boston · Berlin

Foreword

Teresa Andresen

"Landscape Architecture Europe" is new. It is the first issue of a new triennial edition addressed to professionals in Europe and in other parts of the world as well as to those who are interested in landscapes and in the profession of landscape architecture. The profession in Europe still has various specific characteristics within the different countries but the practice will tend to become more homogenous with the impact of European policies on our landscape, as mobility increases and social, cultural and economic standards tend to become more alike. Landscape architects have the competences to meet the challenges required for the building of a new European landscape that will demonstrate the testimony of a continent of many cultures and environments and of the diversity of the art of landscape making. Europe is becoming an area with a very broad and diverse community that calls for innovation in the creation of the new European rural landscape, of accessible and safe leisure landscapes, of enhanced Natura 2000 landscapes that effectively promote our natural and cultural heritage, qualified infrastructures and a more sustainable urban landscape.

"Landscape Architecture Europe" is a collective work. It has been created not by an isolated editorial office but by a group of professionals from diverse European countries and cultural contexts who had met and discussed intensively before publishing what they think demonstrates the European approaches to landscape architecture. In this respect the book is representative of the European profession. It shows more than beautiful and attractive places for people, because it reflects a careful understanding of the landscape and site surroundings, a respect for the natural environment and a consistent way of thinking of the primacy of the well-being of the users.

The European Foundation for Landscape Architecture (EFLA) has a significant interest in the promotion of continuing publication of "Landscape Architecture Europe", a project that in the future will become more and more representative of a Europe that is joined together while at the same time expanding eastwards. This edition offers an opportunity for cross-over information, and for an exchange of landscape approaches. An exchange that respects cultural differences, understands the importance of interdisciplinary aspects, and, finally, has the capacity to evolve.

The European Foundation for Landscape Architecture (EFLA) expresses its gratitude to the Netherlands Architecture Fund for its indispensable financial support for such a collective initiative, and also to those enthusiastic professionals from various countries in Europe who spent so much time, talent and effort on the creation of this book as a mental creation based on a common understanding of European landscape.

Teresa Andresen

Landscape architect, head of the Oporto School of Landscape Architecture, Portugal
President of the European Foundation for Landscape Architecture (EFLA)

Meto J. Vroom

This book is largely the result of the effort and enthusiasm of a number of landscape architects from different European countries, who collected a large number of projects from all over Europe, selected a number of them, edited texts and wrote essays, all of which make up the content of this book. It finds its roots in the Dutch Yearbook on Landscape Architecture and Town Planning, which has proved to be a successful publication and has functioned during the last twelve years as a source of information on the state of the art in the Netherlands. At the same time, it has also served as a benchmark for standards of design quality, in terms of three-dimensional composition, of connection with time and place, of graphics and implementation, all this on scales varying from the local to the regional.

The task of selecting a number of designs that simultaneously meet certain standards and represent various backgrounds and currents within a certain country may take much discussion and a concentrated effort on the part of a jury. The same project undertaken on a European scale, however, is a more complex matter. Landscape architecture in Europe may have been influenced by developments elsewhere, but it still remains largely based on national culture, on national legislation and economy, and on regional topography and climate all of which create significant differences in the nature of design products.

A first single book of a triennial edition cannot fulfil the aim to collect those designs in Europe that are of interest in terms of professional standards and also stimulate the imagination of the reader, that show the state of the art and at the same time represent the work of landscape architects all over Europe. Neither the number of designs collected from all over Europe in the particular period from 2001 to 2004, nor the capacity of one volume that can present no more than about forty examples, allow the producers of this book to achieve both aims simultaneously. This does not mean we will not succeed in this effort. The reader will have to be patient and wait until the time when a series of successive issues has appeared before a cross-section of designs that can be called landscape architecture from all over Europe is represented. Let this be soon!

Meto J. Vroom

Professor emeritus of the Landscape Architecture Chair at Wageningen University, the Netherlands
Chairman of the Landscape Architecture Europe Foundation (LAE)

Contents

Essays

Fieldwork

Lisa Diedrich

The most urgent question today is certainly about the city. That is because cities are growing, everywhere, increasingly rapidly, almost automatically. There is no going back. But how do we want to make our cities? How can we urbanize the planet in a way that is fit for human beings, that conserves resources and that is sustainable? This question is so global that it has no answer. Neither economists nor sociologists have a remedy at hand; neither traffic engineers nor spatial planners can extract a magic formula from their research, even less a worldwide solution – after all, Lagos has nothing to do with the Netherlands' Randstad, and Shanghai is not at all like Milan.

That is why it may seem strange for a book about a design discipline – and in fact urban design – such as landscape architecture to have the title of Fieldwork on its cover. The sound reminds one of agriculture, potatoes, Thanksgiving. It smells of fresh hay and chicken shit. The mind's eye sees hedgerows running up and down rolling hills, plane trees bordering a country road, warping dams lining the Rhine as it flows through the willows of the Gelderland. Tempi passati? Not really, for this was exactly where, on a terrace over the Rhine in the university town of Wageningen, several European landscape architects tired of the constant asking about global issues met to make a fresh start on a local level in January and February of 2005. From the point of view of their discipline, they ventured an answer for Europe, an answer for a part of the planet that has been shaped by human hands for millennia, by agriculture, pasturing, road-building, the construction of cities, and the resulting customs – to cut a long story short, by human culture. It is not on virgin land that Europeans today are developing their cities, but on former farmland that has left its traces on the surface of the earth just as much as in the legal codes of the societies and in the minds of the people. The specifically European answer to the question of how to urbanize is therefore as follows: we are working in the fields and with the fields. It is not the same as for urban and landscape planning in the Siberian tundra or in the Californian desert.

Two essays testify to this fact in the present book. The geo-botanist Hansjörg Küster of Hannover describes the development of European landscape as the history of landscape design, from the first Neolithic farmers to today's builders of ICE railway tracks. The Milanese university lecturer Lionella Scazzosi explains in her essay how this landscape in the suburbs of European metropolises can be developed in various ways to meet the requirements of today's uses, budgets and political strategies without forgetting yesterday's heritage. Certainly, her appeal to understand landscape as a palimpsest is not easy to implement. It demands a strategic commitment of the landscape architectural profession that goes far beyond drawing plans – for instance, to making its voice heard in public.

The willows of Gelderland spreading at the feet of this publication's initiators merely stand pars pro toto for the many other agricultural landscapes of Europe that, with the expertise of landscape architects, could be developed somewhat better into urban landscapes that are fit for human beings, that conserve resources and that are sustainable. The fact that the book began here of all places has to do with its background. Here, immediately facing the material to be designed, in view of the landscape, was where a group of European professionals from EFLA circles founded the Landscape Architecture Europe Foundation. Their aim was to publish specifically European answers in a book – knowing full well that you can only intervene if you disseminate ideas and pictures. Knowing full well, too, that memorable examples of European landscapes can become icons and influence development. For instance, the way the photo of the forest garden by Sven Markelius at his own villa in Kevinge once became the manifesto of the Scandinavian landscape concept of the postwar era, or the pictures of the pre-Olympic squares and parks in Barcelona inspired a new beginning in urban open space design of the late 1980s. The important thing to remember is that the specialists banded together in the Landscape Architecture Europe Foundation do not want to publish theoretical treatises on landscape but to provide insights into the thinking and working of landscape architects. Their point is to publicize the practical work on and with landscape, the "fieldwork".

The fact that ideas and pictures travelled throughout Europe and generated new ideas in the course of recent history is demonstrated vividly in the essay by the Copenhagen university lecturer Malene Hauxner published here. Forms, even styles, originated in Helsinki and were reflected in Lisbon and vice versa. They went from east to west as well. In his essay the Dutch landscape architect Gertjan Jobse, whose professional practice caused him to end up in Poland, explains what kind of soil European ideas land on in the "east"– which is not at all the east but actually the centre of Europe. It always was and now is more than ever. This is what people in Poland, the Czech Republic, the Slovak Republic and Romania emphasize. Jobse has brought their thoughts and opinions on European landscape along for those who are curious about the profession in an expanded Europe. Curiosity – that is the future. In order to clarify the profession's point of departure into this future, the initiators of this book wanted to allow the people they took as examples a hearing. In fact, the European profession is so young that we can still interview its pioneers in person. Karin Helms did exactly that. The educational director of the Ecole Nationale Supérieure du Paysage in Versailles portrays two prominent landscape architects in this book who developed their profiles in the presence of their respective intellectual fathers and gave the profession extremely vital roots.

Fieldwork is always hard physical work. That is what the jury of this book were prepared for. Appointed by the foundation, the group of internationally operating landscape architects from Denmark, the Netherlands, Great Britain, France and Spain met to select a good forty projects from over 500 entries on two weekends. The place for the meeting could not have been better chosen: the almost fully renovated "Schip van Blaauw", a Wageningen University building that the Landscape Architecture Europe Foundation had just moved into. Here the landscape architects set up another construction site: that of the book, of a truly European book. One thing about construction sites is that they are redolent of fresh starts; they instil courage for the new. The members of the jury and the editorial staff were strangers to each other but they all loved courage and fresh starts. Thus, in the course of all-day and all-evening discussions, they created the spirit of approaches, attitudes and cultural backgrounds that this book now attests to. Hardly anyone knew any of the others before – hardly anyone would want to do without the others today. A network of kindred spirits from all over Europe, a collective of fellow players developed of which one alone would never

constitute Europe but together they display the multifaceted European world of ideas. This composite of characters and subjects is perhaps the most important building block for a representative European publication on landscape architecture.

The former lecture hall of "Schip van Blaauw" served as a provisional conference room. The jury and editorial staff sat around a long table replacing the professorial lectern in front of the rows of seats. The rows were empty but it felt as though landscape architects from all over Europe were sitting in those seats and listening to the discussions. From time to time the project presentations they had submitted lay there, spread out over the rows for better visibility. They seemed to have faces – reserved, boasting, delicate, pale, dark, frustrating or fascinating – and, like people,

they moved from the rows onto the jury's table, off again if they were rejected and back again if selected.

According to the democratic principle of not making a preliminary selection from among the entries, the jury was shown everything. Thus these colleagues saw an entire spectrum, according to Michael van Gessel, from "dreadfully crude and insensitive to so outstanding that we gasped with envy that we had not thought of that brilliant idea ourselves!" Robert Camlin expected "the shock of the new" from all different corners of Europe and was disappointed to find relatively many "familiar responses to familiar types of programme". Maria Goula finds that the practice of CAD drawing has in fact contributed to making project presentations look the same everywhere – another small step and will

building be the same everywhere too? The projects submitted mainly reflect landscape architecture's classic fields of activity: parks, gardens, public open spaces, and the grounds around buildings. In many of the projects the jury recognized the influence of certain trends; many exhibited "a touch of Barcelona", as Michael van Gessel put it: endless playing with forms but no real substance. Others turned out to be commissioned architecture, "corporate landscape architecture" – expensive, perfect, but utterly boring. What the jury found interesting was the cross-border aspect of many a project: French landscape architects building in Greece, Dutch in Germany, Argentinians in Ireland. What it missed was landscape architecture projected from a regional planning or otherwise strategic point of view. Even if we assume that few such projects were submitted, we cannot help getting the impression that

landscape architects between Oslo and Palermo have little influence on initiating major changes in spatial planning in cities, in the country, or in suburbia. Regardless of whether the raw material for the present book is representative or not, landscape architecture's campaign is imminent...

Before the jury came together, each member had reviewed all the projects at home. During the meetings, the jurors discussed each project both as such and from the point of view of publication. Each juror then gave each project a plus, a minus or a question mark. If the plusses were in the majority (3 out of 5 votes), the project remained in the race; if the question marks were in the majority, it was put aside for further discussion; if the minuses were in the majority, it was rejected. By the end of the first weekend, 35 plus and 45 question-mark projects were left on the rows in the lecture hall, 80 projects in all. On the second weekend the jurors pored over the question-mark projects once more and, after intense discussion, gave eight of them a plus. Finally they pondered all the plus projects together and selected the 43 published here.

The perseverance this process demanded of the jurors is easy to imagine. But this was not about fitness training. It was about evaluating landscape projects and exchanging reactions upon looking at them only in the form of drawings, plans, texts and photos. Henri Bava describes this as the search for what is sound, true and just. "The jurors get an impression from the information submitted; they determine the divergences and differences in their assessments and establish their positions in the group... until suddenly everything about a project is clear, self-evident, sound, unanimous. It is like playing a piece of music together." Yet while soundness is immediately apparent in music, a project requires time for discussion, time for the players to be able to question something that a photo may conceal but that gaining a perspective on the proposal with respect to the site, climate and context may bring to light. The jury is fascinated, says Bava, when it discovers the author's leitmotiv, his approach, when his music emerges, when the jury can accompany the author for a few moments in his playing, joining in admiringly, even identifying with him. "Unlike architecture, which challenges a site, landscape projects are more comprehensive interventions – like transplants that have to 'take' in a site. Hence a project is sound not when its forms are particularly pure but when it 'takes' as a transplant." With many a project the landscape architect's input, or the working process itself, is more appealing than the result. Soundness becomes a very personal matter; it lies in a colleague's approach to his project. Ultimately, finding these sensitive personal touches is what earns the most respect from the jury, for, according to Henri Bava, here is "an individual faced with the concert of the world".

The jury was doubtful about many of the projects. While some aspects may have been attractive, doubt about the soundness of the whole outweighed them. If the information provided did not allow going into

greater depth, the jury risked making a mistake. Mistakes cause insecurity – the project was rejected. In a selection such as this, Stig Andersson believes there can be no right or wrong but only the joint verdict of a group of specialists about the how and why of one or more projects. A landscape architect responds to the question the landscape asks him, and if that question does not correspond with the question the client asks him, a conflict will ensue, or even a battle. This battle is evident in many a project, thinks Stig Andersson, and therefore the verdict sometimes refers as much to the client's aspirations as to the planner's abilities. Andersson's criterion for the publication of a project is simply, "If it has nothing to do with wanting to change the world, then it should not appear in this book". It makes no difference to him whether he is discussing tiny projects or projects of vast dimensions, architectural plans or engineering plans – what matters is to understand and appreciate the landscape architectural idea. The jury agrees with him that the projects in the book should not be organized according to categories such as parks and gardens, public squares and places, and regional plans. As though each category called for a different design approach... nonsense.

Again and again the jury talked about landscape as a part of memory, a piece of intellectual property. Maria Goula comments that projects shaping water, vegetation and other natural elements into a memorable and remembered picture of landscape attracted special attention, "The majority of the selected projects were distinguished by the fact that their authors found a particular way of either inscribing the project into the memory of the site or interpreting the history, memory and nature of each site in a radical and profound way." Perhaps what makes a project stand out even in a globalized world is its character, suggests Goula. This character comes about when landscape architects deal with common problems using more or less the same instruments in very specific local conditions. Sophisticated non-design is what Michael van Gessel calls such projects. "They look so appropriate that they do not look designed at all. Reserved, restrained. On the other hand, there was also a preference for remarkable designs, spaces with feeling, with powerful expressiveness".

The jury was not always in agreement; there was controversy. Robert Camlin is pleased with the projects now collected in the book. He is also pleased that they include some he had not favoured – simply for the lively debate they prompted. Camlin welcomes the fact that ambitious young designers stand beside the old masters of landscape architecture in this book because, as he says, "A lively profession needs both its heroes and its exuberant youth. If I were to lean in a particular direction it would be to the latter, but then I approach my doddering middle age and need to be reminded of what it was like to be fearless!"

The members of the jury do not presume to have formulated or illustrated a specifically European design approach. Instead, in Michael van Gessel's words, they found that sobriety, restrained interventions, enhancement of the beauty of both living and dead material, sheer craftsmanship, playing with the dimension of time, subtlety, and special kinds of poetry could all be found in these projects: "Their freedom gives me the energy to go beyond the limits of my inventiveness and to keep producing new ideas." In Europe one has to cross boundaries to do so. And even though the first selection of projects to come out of this cross-border activity does not yet represent the entire European profession, outstanding works and thoughts emerge from the pages of this book and move us. Thus they inject new power into building, into everyday European life and into fieldwork.

Mapping an identity

Robert Holden

Europe is geographically a peninsular; it is a western promontory of Eurasia. In reality, ideas of Europe are primarily cultural, rather than geographical. If considered as a continent it is the world's second smallest in area, with a size of about 10 million square kilometres, but in terms of population it is the third largest continent after Asia and Africa. Europe's population of around 815 million is about 12 percent of the world total.

In the 20th century, most maps showed Europe as bounded to the north by the Arctic Ocean, to the west by the Atlantic, to the south by the Mediterranean and Black Seas and to the East by the Urals, Caspian Sea and River Emba. But in the nineteenth century many maps excluded the Caucasus and showed a boundary along the Urals and Rivers Volga and Don. Now the Council of Europe embraces the whole of Turkey, the Caucasian Republics and Russia. Curiously, Cyprus, which culturally is seen as part of Europe, is geographically clearly part of Asia.

Ideas of Europe

The point of this is that Europe is primarily a cultural construct: ideas of Europe and European identity change. For Homer, *Europa* was the mythical Phoenician princess abducted by Zeus (in the form of a bull) and taken to Crete, and who gave birth to King Minos. Later the word was applied to mainland Greece and by 500 BC its meaning extended to lands to the north. The term is derived from *eruys* (broad) and *ops* (face), though some authorities point to Akkadian origins in *ereba,* which means sunset. From an Asian point of view the sun sets in the lands to the West. Linguistically, too, the majority of European languages are Indo-European and Europe's main religions originated in the Middle East. One can see the last three millennia of ideas of Europe as a part of the development of the wider Western Eurasian culture beginning with the Mesopotamian civilizations, which emerged before 3000 BC.

Irish landscape architect Robert Camlin points out that Europe last had a common currency in Celtic times when salt was the means of exchange from the Danube to Gaul and Britannia. Historically, European ideas of democracy came from Greece while the Roman Empire influenced the economy and culture of the whole of Europe. Politically, it extended north of the Danube and Rhine and to Scotland. Ideas of a European identity founded on Rome spread via Byzantium and the Orthodox Church to Russia and via the Franks to the Holy Roman Empire. For orthodox Christendom Moscow was the Third Rome. Cultural ideas of a common European identity were fostered by the use of Latin as the *lingua franca* of cultural and scientific exchange until the 19th century.

The steamship companies and railways of the 19th century fostered communication and travel. The Grand Tour of the 18th century, which lasted a year or so, was superseded by summer vacations – English prime ministers from Gladstone in the 19th century to Churchill, one

hundred years later, favoured the French Riviera for summer holidays, while Tony Blair now holidays in Tuscany. In the early 19th century the Emperor Napoleon united Europe and codified its Roman systems of law, but his empire led to reactions against a single European identity and fostered the nineteenth century rise of the nation state. Larousse's *Grand Dictionnaire* of 1870 says in its consideration of Europe: "Under the Caesars and under Charlemagne Europe, already ancient, had its own identity so one was Asian, African or European. However, under the first Napoleon Europe lost its identity, we are French, English, Italian, Greek, Russian, etc.: we are not European."

The history of the European landscape as a wider common identity is *par excellence* one of cultural expression, central political direction or of economic dictat. Landscape reflects society and its history. The evidence of Celtic field patterns is found in the mountainous west whether in Britanny, Cornwall or Wales and recalls their farming systems and social organization. The remains of Roman *latifundia*, still survive in England as well as in Italy, and Roman roads are found in the Highlands of Scotland. Dutch engineers directed drainage in the 17th century Fenlands of East Anglia. The Emperor Napoleon followed Henri IV in spreading *arbres d'alignement* along the roads of France. Hitler's Germany was a favoured place for landscape architects who wished to restructure the Greater Reich. Stalin and his political disciple Walter Ulbricht brought *Populus* to the avenues and *prospekti* of Moscow and the roads of Eastern Germany, and collectivisation extended throughout much of Central and Eastern Europe. Today the European Union's Common Agricultural Policy determines the form of the landscape of its 25 member countries and is reshaping the agriculture of the 2004 Accession Countries.

Pan-Europeanism

In the 20th century, pan-Europeanism was an ambition and partial achievement of both fascism and communism. Following the Second World War, and in reaction to a history of centuries of European warfare between national states, trans-national European institutions were established. These were concurrent with the growth of global institutions such as those of the United Nations. European bodies include the Council of Europe (1949), Comecon (1955), the Western European Union (1955) and the Common Market or European Economic Community (1957) – now the European Union. To quote the *Great Soviet Encyclopedia* of 1970 (Macmillan English translation published 1975): "The European Economic Community represents a new phenomenon… characteristic of the monopoly phase of capitalism. It reflects an objective towards internationalisation of economic relations and capital and elimination of narrow national boundaries."

Today one would term this tendency globalization and access to mapping is access to information, hence the significance of freedom of access to mapping information.

More recently and in response many European interest groups and NGOs have been set up to represent environmental concerns (such as the European Environment Bureau or the European Public Health Alliance). Also federations of professional associations have been established such as Liaison Committee for Town Planners in the EEC (later the European Council for Town Planners) in the late 1960s, the European Foundation for Landscape Architecture (EFLA) in 1989, the Architects' Council of Europe in 1990 and in 1991 the European Forum of Medical Associations. These aim to represent their professions at a European level.

Maps as evidence of identity

Maps are evidence of how Europe is seen. Look at 19th century maps of Europe and one sees a land described in terms of rivers and mountain ranges. Mapping is vital to political, economic and social management of resources. French mapping of the 18th century reflected the power and control of the French state. One of the first tasks of the British Empire on taking over India from the East India Company in the 1850s was to map it. Maps are a way of conquering and controlling the world. In most countries mapping was a role for the army, just as hydrographical surveys were a way to naval power. The British naval supremacy of the 19th century was built on hydrographical mapping. Currently the European Union and the European Space Agency are vying with the US government and NASA on issues such as global monitoring, repeating the competition between, say, the British, Spanish, French and Dutch admiralties during the 17th and 18th centuries.

In the 1970s plans such as the 1966 Dutch *Tweede Nota over de Ruimtelijke Ordening* (Second Note on Physical Planning), which showed a context covering northern France and south-east England, were remarkable at the time for considering such an international context. Since the 1990s, and in response to trans-national policies across Europe, there has been a growth of trans-national mapping and land data management systems. The development of satellite data access and use of Geographic Information Systems has revolutionised the process of data collection and presentation. Consequently maps can become a developing, changing and constantly updated tool, accessible to all. In the 1990s use of satellite based global positioning enabled production of mapping databases free of ground triangulation. Since 1985 the European Union has been looking at landscape change in Europe through several projects, PELCOM and CORINE. The latter developed an inventory of biophysical land cover, a digital version of which was published in 2004 by the European Environment Agency. Further work of this nature has been taken up in the European Union's INSPIRE project, which has been running since 2002 (see block captions for more details of these various initiatives).

The European Landscape Convention and LANMAP

The Council of Europe, with a membership of 46 countries, is much wider than the European Union. Almost all European countries, including Iceland and Turkey are members, except Byelorussia, the Vatican City and Kazakhstan (which extends west of the Urals and the River Emba). Indeed, the membership of Russia extends this definition of Europe to Vladivostok. The Council's European Landscape Convention of 2000 is very significant in that it is the first international agreement to cover the *whole* of the territory of participating states. It commits countries to identify and assess all their own landscapes (Article 6) whether good, bad or indifferent.

In this respect work such as LANMAP developed by the Wageningen based Alterra Research Institute in the Netherlands, is interesting. It aims to apply a variety of sources such as CORINE, the European Soil Map and PELCOM to a comprehensive pan-European mapping system specifically in order to meet the needs of the European Landscape Convention. Most countries undertake land use planning both nationally and locally. For example, in Germany, the Federal Land Use Planning Law (*Bundes-Raumordnungsgesetz, ROG*) is a general planning framework to form an overall framework for each region's land use planning law and executive action.

Landscape and Land Use Planning

In many countries, land use planning has had a limited influence on land use change. Controls on agriculture practice are most often found in north-western Europe, including Denmark, the Netherlands, and Germany where pressure on the land resource from competing demands for development, recreation, forestry and agriculture is intense. Alterra intend that LANMAP assists with:

· planning policy: essentially long-term frameworks for guiding and prompting development including land use change, infrastructure and housing development etc.
· planning controls: regulatory procedures and rules over changes in land use, for example agricultural set-aside and afforestation of farmland, development, nature conservation and flood control.

In view of the extension of the European Union into Central Europe, effective planning, and the means to enable it, is necessary if the Common Agricultural Policy is not to have a totally destructive effect on rural infrastructure, wildlife and landscape quality.

Similarly these techniques should allow easy exchange of information and comparison across Europe. City region landscape planning is well developed in Germany and indeed in France, but is limited elsewhere. LANMAP could be a means to make the Île de France planning process accessible and comparable for, say, London planners.

Participation

The internet fosters participation and free access to such land mapping information. Hence a project such as Gigateway in the UK is welcome. Gigateway is a free web service aimed at increasing awareness of, and access to, geospatial information in the UK. One uses a data locator to find out what geographic datasets exist, and an area search to find out more about where you live. The data directory is intended to help locate organizations, which supply geographic data, products and services and, in a sense, this is an attempt to provide free information and make it publicly accessible. If this sort of free access can be extended across the European Union and across the wider Europe then the internet could serve to democratize the planning and use of land. No longer would mapping be a way to control but rather it would become a way to encourage participation.

This book contains a selection of projects chosen by an independent jury. Interestingly the selection does not fully represent the scope of landscape architecture as there is little in the way of landscape planning in this book. *Landscape Architecture Europe* is a continuing project, which aims to represent all aspects of landscape architecture including landscape planning in a series of such yearbooks. As part of this work, data resources, such as those described above, will play a vital role in the future evolution of much landscape planning and design. This essay is an attempt to place this first *tranche* of landscape projects within the wider context of growing opportunities for landscape architecture within Europe's culturally significant landscapes.

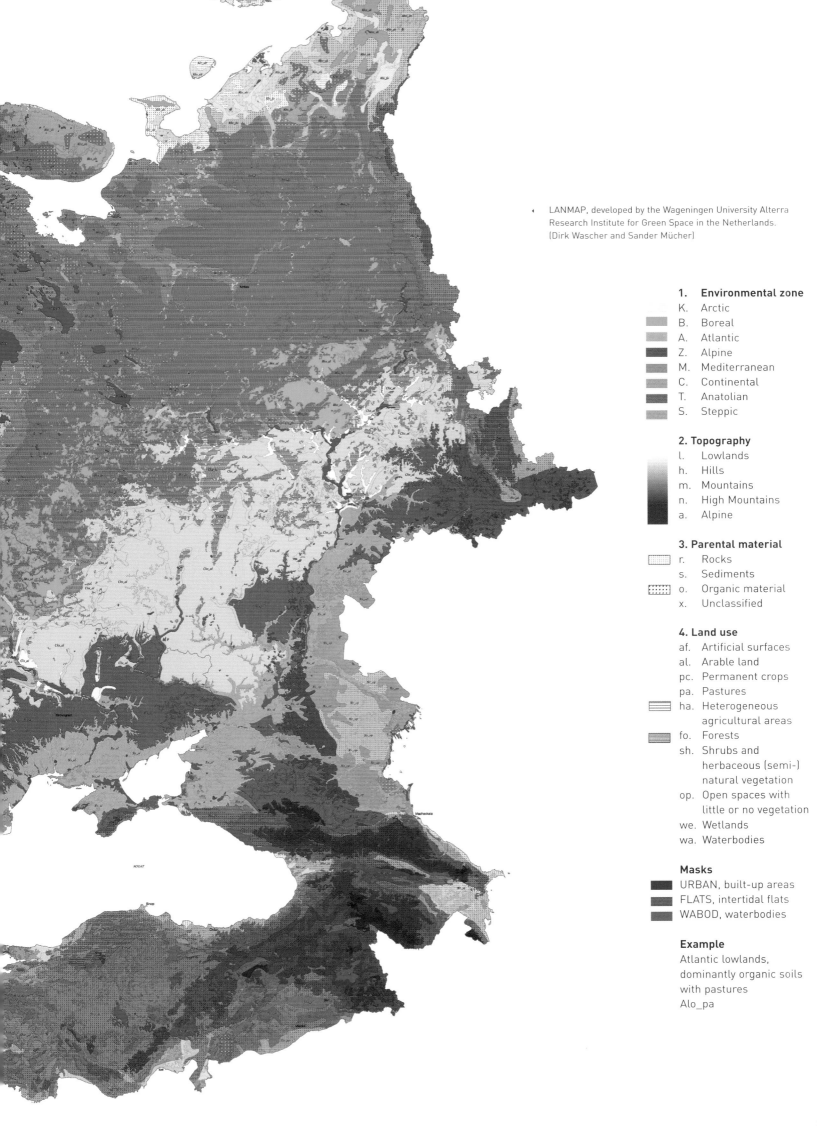

LANMAP, developed by the Wageningen University Alterra
Research Institute for Green Space in the Netherlands.
(Dirk Wascher and Sander Mücher)

1. Environmental zone
K. Arctic
B. Boreal
A. Atlantic
Z. Alpine
M. Mediterranean
C. Continental
T. Anatolian
S. Steppic

2. Topography
l. Lowlands
h. Hills
m. Mountains
n. High Mountains
a. Alpine

3. Parental material
r. Rocks
s. Sediments
o. Organic material
x. Unclassified

4. Land use
af. Artificial surfaces
al. Arable land
pc. Permanent crops
pa. Pastures
ha. Heterogeneous
    agricultural areas
fo. Forests
sh. Shrubs and
    herbaceous (semi-)
    natural vegetation
op. Open spaces with
    little or no vegetation
we. Wetlands
wa. Waterbodies

Masks
URBAN, built-up areas
FLATS, intertidal flats
WABOD, waterbodies

Example
Atlantic lowlands,
dominantly organic soils
with pastures
Alo_pa

▾ LANMAP uses Geographic Information Systems to present data sources dealing with climate, topography, parent material and land use.

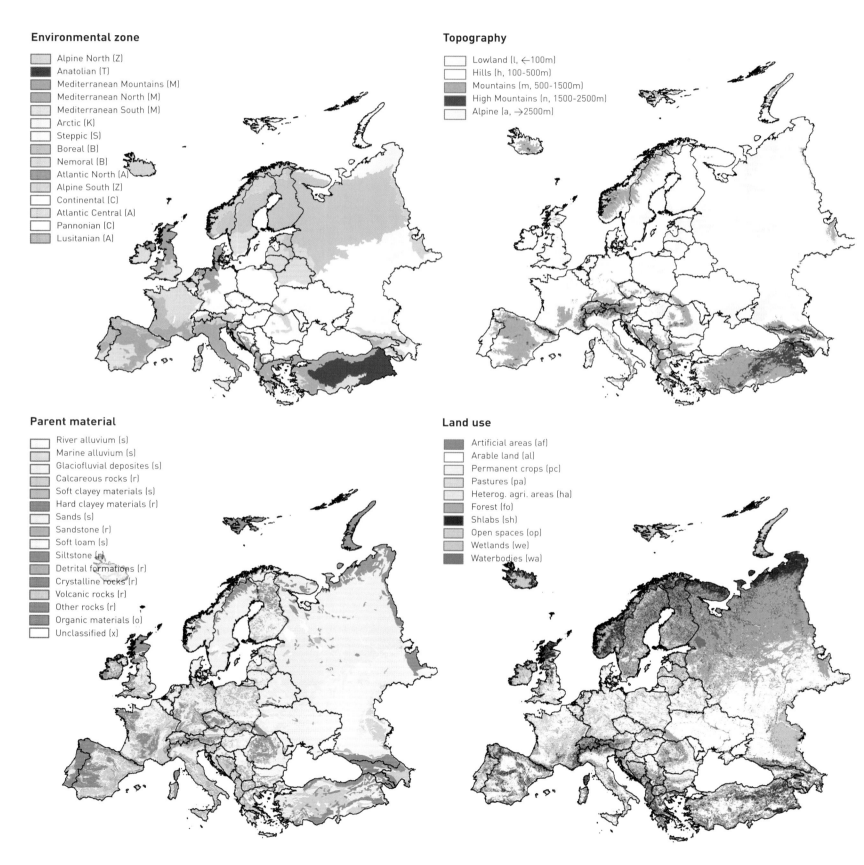

Environmental zone

- Alpine North (Z)
- Anatolian (T)
- Mediterranean Mountains (M)
- Mediterranean North (M)
- Mediterranean South (M)
- Arctic (K)
- Steppic (S)
- Boreal (B)
- Nemoral (B)
- Atlantic North (A)
- Alpine South (Z)
- Continental (C)
- Atlantic Central (A)
- Pannonian (C)
- Lusitanian (A)

Topography

- Lowland (l, ←100m)
- Hills (h, 100-500m)
- Mountains (m, 500-1500m)
- High Mountains (n, 1500-2500m)
- Alpine (a, →2500m)

Parent material

- River alluvium (s)
- Marine alluvium (s)
- Glaciofluvial deposites (s)
- Calcareous rocks (r)
- Soft clayey materials (s)
- Hard clayey materials (r)
- Sands (s)
- Sandstone (r)
- Soft loam (s)
- Siltstone (r)
- Detrital formations (r)
- Crystalline rocks (r)
- Volcanic rocks (r)
- Other rocks (r)
- Organic materials (o)
- Unclassified (x)

Land use

- Artificial areas (af)
- Arable land (al)
- Permanent crops (pc)
- Pastures (pa)
- Heterog. agri. areas (ha)
- Forest (fo)
- Shlabs (sh)
- Open spaces (op)
- Wetlands (we)
- Waterbodies (wa)

European Land and Landscape Mapping Systems – an overview

PELCOM (Pan-European Land Use and Land Cover Monitoring)
This project aimed at establishing a one kilometre pan-European land cover database that could be updated frequently. It was based on work that began at RIVM (the Dutch National Institute for Public Health and the Environment) in 1992. The database was based on the integrative use of multi-spectral and multi-temporal one-kilometre resolution NOAA-AVHRR satellite data and ancillary data. PELCOM was a three-year project under the Environment & Climate section of the European Union's 4th framework Research and Technological Development Programme. The project started in September 1996 and was carried out within an international framework, and was jointly co-ordinated by the Dutch Ministry of Agriculture, Nature Conservation and Fisheries and DLO Winand Staring Centre for Integrated Land, Soil and Water Research, in Wageningen.
http://www.geo-informatie.nl/projects/pelcom/public/index.htm

CORINE
Since 1985 the European Union has been looking at landscape change in Europe using the CORINE inventory of biophysical land cover. The European environment agency first published a digital version of CORINE in 2004. It provides a 44-class nomenclature and is available on a Pan European 250 square metre database which is publicly accessible on
http://dataservice.eea.eu.int/atlas/viewdata/viewpub.asp?id=1.
CORINE covers Austria, Belgium, the Czech Republic, Denmark, Finland, Germany, Greece, Hungary, Ireland, Italy, Luxembourg, the Netherlands, Poland, Portugal, Spain, United Kingdom and even parts of Morocco and Tunisia. The map data covers 44 categories, including agriculture types, abandonment of grassland, ecological regions, soils and biogeographical regions.

INSPIRE PROJECT (Infrastructure For Spatial Information In Europe)
Spatial information in Europe is fragmented, datasets and sources, and even datum levels are uncoordinated. There are gaps in availability, and a lack of harmonization between datasets at different geographical scales and sometimes a duplication of data collection. These problems make it difficult to identify, access and use the available data. INSPIRE was set up by the European Commission in 2002 and the project involves the European Environmental Agency, Eurostat, the Joint Research Centre and the Directorate-General for the Environment of the European Commission.
http://www.ec-gis.org/inspire.

INSPIRE is complementary to other EU policy initiatives, such as the European Union *Directive on the re-use of public sector information* of 2003 which aims to promote open, and if possible free, access to public information.

The aim is to promote the creation of a European spatial information infrastructure that delivers integrated spatial information services to its users. These services should allow users to identify and access spatial or geographical information from a wide range of sources, from the local to the global level, in an inter-operable way for a variety of uses. The users include policy-makers, planners and managers at European, national and local level and citizens and their organizations. Possible services include the visualization of information layers, overlay of information from different sources, spatial and temporal analysis, etc.

LANMAP
LANMAP, developed by the Wageningen University Alterra Research Institute for Green Space in the Netherlands is an interesting further development. It aims to apply a variety of sources such as CORINE, the European Soil Map and PELCOM to a comprehensive pan European mapping system specifically in order the meet the needs of the European Landscape Convention. It uses Geographic Information Systems to present data sources dealing with:
· climate
· topography (using the US/UNEP GTOPO30 Global Topographic Data) *(http://edcdaac.usgs.gov/gtopo30/gtopo30.asp)*
· parent material/Ecological stand conditions (European Soil Map) *(http://eusoils.jrc.it/*)
· land use/land cover (CORINE, PELCOM or Pan European Land Use and Land Cover Monitoring *(http://www.geo-informatie.nl/projects/pelcom/)* and the Global Land Cover project or GLC 2000. *(http://www.fao.org/gtos/news24.html)*

So far it has developed some 350 landscape types. The aim of LANMAP is to provide a European landscape map for regional, national and international landscape and spatial planning concerned with the implementation of European legislation, trans-boundary projects and the wider integration of national or local planning policy. For further information *http://www.alterra.wur.nl/UK.*

What you see is what you made – landscape as a cultural product

Hansjörg Küster

The historical landscapes of Europe are one of the continent's most distinctive features. A product of agricultural activity and development, they shape the special character of each region. One of the future's most important tasks will be conveying the uniqueness of these European landscapes and educating resident and visiting populations about their cultural value. Each landscape needs to be understood and appreciated from a historical perspective so that, for example, people understand why dikes, agricultural terraces, and canals were built for drainage, or why heath lands were expanded and then curbed by agricultural reforms. In Europe, there is a long cultural tradition of creating and shaping landscapes, an aspect that cannot be emphasized enough. Europe is not a land of dynamic nature, but rather, a land shaped and designed. In Europe, the economic and creative forces of agriculture transformed nature into human landscapes.

The Origin of Agriculture: ex oriente lux

The mountains of the Middle East are the world's most important region for the origin of cultivated plants and domestic animals: wheat and barley, peas and lentils, flax and olive trees, cattle, sheep and goats all originate from this area. There is no other part of the world where farmers have found such a large variety of fauna and flora for their use. Yet, agricultural crises have always been an observable fact in the Middle East: in many places water was not continuously available; in other places, irrigation resulted in an increase in the soil's salinity.

In the regions bordering immediately to the west of the Middle East, farming and animal husbandry were much less affected by crises. Over the course of more than 7,000 years, Europe became the only region in the world where the tillage of the fields and livestock breeding was not disrupted by periodically recurring problems. Speculation is that the culture of Europe could therefore assume a dominant role world-wide. In most parts of Europe, the climate is favourable to agriculture. As in the regions where cultivated plants originate, a mild rainy season conducive to the growth of foliage, fruit, seeds and roots is a common climatic characteristic. In the Middle East, rains fall during the winter, whereas in Europe they occur during the early summer. In the subsequent dry period, grains can ripen. There are always dry summers in the Middle East, but farmers in Europe hope for dry east winds in the middle of summer, with the harvest season usually occurring sometime between July and September. Rainfall throughout the year produces the grass that is turned into fodder for animals.

The Gulf Stream carries warm water from the Caribbean to the coasts of Western Europe and on further towards the North. Nowhere else in the world is it possible to till the soil so close to the pole, even north of the Arctic Circle. Europe's inland seas – the Mediterranean, the Black and the Baltic Sea – create a mild and equable climate. During the summer, winds coming in from the seas cool off inland temperatures; during autumn and winter, the waters store warmer temperatures, thus preventing heavy frosts in the countries along these coasts.

During the various ice ages, large parts of the continent were covered with glaciers. Big masses of ice ground the rocks of Scandinavia, Finland and the high mountain regions into rubble and transported the debris far across the continent. After the ice melted, huge stones (called boulders), sand, and fine-grained gravel were left behind. The fine particles contained all the minerals that plants need for optimal growth. Winds removed fine material from the rubble and dropped it immediately in front of or between mountainous regions, thus creating fertile and rock-free loess areas, which eventually evolved into the core regions of European agriculture.

The Creation of the Agri-Cultural Landscape

Conditions for the introduction of agriculture in Europe were particularly favourable. People still needed, however, to break new ground, as it were, before they could sow their grains and pasture their animals. After the most recent Ice Age, the fertile soil and mild climate supported the expansion of forests throughout Europe. These woodlands constantly changed their shape and appearance. Initially, pine and birch trees were predominant in many parts of Europe, later followed by hazelnut in the western parts of the continent and fir trees in the east. In the north-east, pine and birch trees survived for the longest period, in some cases into the present day. In many places, oaks and elms, ash and linden trees formed mixed forests. In contrast, beeches and hornbeams were still confined to small areas in Southern Europe. These species did not expand beyond their regional habitats until after large parts of Europe had come under the farmer's plough.

The forests were cleared; agriculture was gaining ground. Tree trunks became houses; branches and twigs became the firewood necessary for cooking and baking, in addition to being used as raw material for all sorts of tools and instruments. Once the forest was cleared, the soil could be tilled. And establishing a field in close proximity to the remaining woods had positive effects on farming: during summer days, cool breezes brought moisture from the forest into the fields, while during spring and autumn, temperatures beneath the trees remained relatively warm so that mild air currents from the groves kept the frost at bay when the land started to cool down.

Over hundreds and thousands of years, people even learned to turn those lands that originally did not support trees into agri-cultural landscapes. Before they could be used to grow grains, the woodless lands along the coast needed to be diked. People drained moors and swamps, and irrigated the steppes. Without such measures, that is, without preparing, transforming and shaping the land, the development of European agriculture would have been impossible, as would the establishment of permanent settlements. The farming village became the core and focal point of the landscape. Settlements were laid out in such a manner that fields and pastures were located nearby. Starting a village halfway up the slope of a valley was ideal since the foot of the valley faced the constant danger of flooding. In addition, the soil at the bottom of the slope was stony, water having washed away the finer sediments in the course of the valley's geological formation, while the upper parts of the slope still contained sand and clay deposits – the soil necessary for tilling. Ploughshares and hoes were far less likely to break because the fertile ground here was almost completely free of rocks, and consequently, grain harvests were plentiful. Traditionally, farmers built their houses and villages in so-called ecotopal border zones, i.e. places located between the relatively even and smooth arable lands on the slopes and those low-lying parts of the valley that served as pasturelands for feeding and watering animals.

It was not necessary to clear the forest for livestock. Domestic animals found plenty of food in the woods. Over time, however, groves thinned out because animals not only ate grass and herbage but also foliage from trees and shrubs, and they consumed saplings before they could mature. When old trees died off, there were not enough young trees to replace them. Over the centuries, with the continuation of this form of grazing, once-thick forests became open heath lands.

The diversity of Europe's Agri-Cultural Lands

During the first millennia after the last Ice Age, when Europe was still largely covered by forests, the continent must have looked rather uniform and monotonous. Oak tree forests stretched all the way from the Mediterranean to the Baltic Sea, from Ireland to the Balkans. But these

◄ The Eifel region in Germany, a mosaic of fields, greenlands and forests. Air streaming out of the forests provides a balanced microclimate.

▾ Polders to the north of Amsterdam, the Netherlands: dykes and drainage systems allow intensive agriculture.

forests grew on soils made of different sediments, some rock-hard, some porous and some chalky. Climatic conditions also varied widely. But perhaps the layers of fine, mineral-rich sand and clay, which winds had deposited all over the continent after the last glacial period, eventually helped to compensate for climatic differences, evening out regional variations. Europe's forests looked different from those in the moderate climes of the Far East and North America: they did not comprise such a broad variety of trees and shrubs. During the Tertiary, Europe also boasted a broad variety of trees, but many of them died out in the cold periods during the Ice Age that followed this geological era. Yet in the Far East and North America, they survived.

It was only when agriculture was introduced and the transformative influence of human culture took hold of Europe that the character of the continent again diversified. Some of the cultivated plants from the Orient's botanical wealth were more suitable for further cultivation along the Mediterranean, others were better suited to the conditions in Central Europe. A stockpile of wheat could be safely stored only in dry regions, which is why wheat was grown around the Mediterranean. In the north, people cultivated wild einkorn, wild emmer and spelt. Related to wheat, these grains are much less susceptible to humidity and, thus, easier to store in moist climates. Olive trees were planted all around the Mediterranean, eventually becoming the signature plant of this region and marking its geographical borders. Like other cultivated plants, the wild ancestors of the olive tree originate in the east, yet the pattern of their dispersion today is a result of human intervention.

The people inhabiting various parts of Europe raised animals of various species. Over the course of time, they bred many different animal races

that became typical for a specific region. Fertile pasture lands fostered cattle breeding, while sheep and goats were easy to keep on less fertile grasslands and on steep and rough terrains. Sheep are content with grass and herbage, goats crop shrubs and bushes and climb trees to nibble off the leaves. Grazing goats caused large-scale destruction of Mediterranean mountain forests. If, in the long run, people wanted to prevent pasture lands from reverting back into forests, they could not depend on sheep alone but needed to add goats to their herds, animals which would eat sprouting shrubs and bushes as well as hard thistles. For similar reasons, many shepherds introduced donkeys into their herds, an animal that also provided a means of transportation, carrying goods from the Mediterranean coasts into the mountains and back. The distance that donkeys carried such goods inland became a measure of the influence of early civilizations on the interior parts of the continent.

Over the course of time, white Charolais cattle became typical of many parts of France. In the mountains, people kept other cattle breeds – grey, spotted and red and white. The small and lightweight Hinterwalds were a cattle breed particularly suitable for the southern German highlands and were found, above all, in the higher altitudes of the Black Forest. The Highland, a breed with straggly hair mostly found in the British Isles, could be kept out in the open all year round. Southern Europe, the limestone mountains of Southern and Central Germany, and the Iberian Peninsula – each of these European regions had its own breed of sheep. A typical pasture animal on the heath lands, which stretched from Portugal to Norway across the western parts of Europe, was the *Heidschnucke*, a moorland sheep that is not really a sheep at all, but a descendant of the mouflon. The *Heidschnucke* grazes on grass and young heather shoots, and forages on young trees and shrubs. The Heidschnucke keeps the

heath lands open. It is an undemanding pasture animal who, unlike other animals, is easily content with tuffed hair grass and heather.

Some European regions are suitable for grazing all year round, particularly the wet and cool areas in the west, along the Atlantic and the North Sea. In the continent's interior, lush mountain pastures can only be found during the summer; during the winter, they disappear under thick blankets of snow. In those regions, animals can only be pastured during the warm season; during the winter, they need to be driven to the lower parts of the valley where they can still find food. Every year, and with changing seasons, herdsmen move their animals to the best pasture grounds. This form of land use is called transhumance. In the Alps and other high mountain areas it is also known as Alpine agriculture or *Almwirtschaft*.

In regions influenced by a continental climate, the amount of annual rain differs from year to year. After a rainfall, animals can graze on lush pastures for a period of time, but must be driven far across the country – to new, lush pastures – during the dry season that follows the rain. The nomads of south-eastern Europe adapted to such a way of life. Living in the steppes and semi-deserts, their pasture animals have moulded the typical character of these landscapes. Nomads – the Lapps and Sami people – also live in the northern parts of the continent. Moving and grazing across the land, their reindeer destroy the vegetation cover. After a herd of reindeer has spent a certain amount of time in one particular location, vegetation needs a recovery period of several years. For this reason, and observing the rhythm of the seasons, reindeer herders are always on the move: in the summer, one finds them in the north, in the winter they are in the warmer south.

What is nature in Europe?

The diversity of landscapes created by people who tilled the soil and raised animals became the continent's "trademark", so much so that many people regard this bucolic world as Europe's "second nature". For many centuries, people visited an Arcadian south, a country of peasants and shepherds, of vineyards, olive groves and small grain fields. But Arcadia was not so much a real destination of travellers as it was a landscape of desire, a place that people living north of the Alps dreamed about, where the landscape offered rather different living conditions. After being overly utilized during the Middle Ages and in the early modern age, much of the soil was depleted. Forests were confined to small residual patches. Farmers took efforts to ensure that their fields produced the largest possible harvests – but without much success. As a consequence, famines ravaged the population again and again. Extensive land reforms begun in the 18th century provided relief. Land use was newly regulated; smaller fields were combined into larger ones. Originally known as merger (because individual fields were merged into larger ones), this method was later called land consolidation (*Flurbereinigung*). At the same time, large common pasture lands that had been used for centuries by herdsmen for their cattle, sheep, goats, and pigs, were now allocated to individual users. Land that remained, or was designated as a community's common property, was termed the green commons. In the English-speaking world, the partitioning of the common lands and their allocation to individual farmers was known as enclosure – small parcels of the green commons were fenced in and surrounded by hedgerows. In England, this measure was decreed by the General Enclosure Act. Now, livestock could be kept on the enclosed parcels without herdsmen. Former herders could now move to the big industrial cities, and young people could go to school. Because of enclosure it was possible to widely introduce general, compulsory education. If people grew hedges instead of building fences, they saved wood, a scarce

◄ A village near Dachau, Upper Bavaria, Germany: greenlands extend below the village; cultivated fields lie on the flat area above the farmhouses.
▾ Agriculturally exploited land near Bergen, Norway: the field to the left of the wall is fertilized; the heath to the right isn't.

commodity; moreover, hedges became an additional source of firewood for the rural population.

Dirt roads were developed into wider country roads with a solid foundation and cover. People dug ditches on both sides of the road so that the rainwater and melted snow and ice could drain away. In addition, they planted trees on both sides of the road. These alley trees protected travellers from being overly exposed to the elements. But trees and ditches also had another function: in previous centuries, coach and wagon drivers often left a well-established lane when it was soggy and started a new, parallel one. This practice had created roads that were up to a hundred metres wide. Now, trees and ditches forced drivers to use existing lanes even when they were hardly passable. As a result, the width of roads was reduced to a tenth of that of medieval ones, and new arable land became available. During the same period, forests were marked off from fields and

grazing land. Livestock, now thriving on intensely used, enclosed pastures, no longer grazed among the trees. As a consequence, forests became thicker again.

Over time, many of Europe's agrarian landscapes were reshaped by these measures. Originally, it was the landed gentry and other rural aristocracy who supported such land reforms. By the 19th century, the land was shaped in ways that are still appreciated and loved by many people today. In these culturally created landscapes, agricultural productivity was higher and what was produced in the rural areas could go to support a growing urban population. Famine became rare. And many developments marked the beginning of what is known today as "the good old days". New cultivated plants came into fashion, among them the profitable potato. Since the 19th century, potatoes and other crops have been easily shipped into cities

by rail. Fruit travelled the same way. Many of the orchards that we perceive as a typical characteristic of rural landscapes today did not come into existence until urban markets were within easy reach. Formerly dependent farmers were liberated and gained access to the capital market. The invention of mineral fertilizers increased agricultural yield, and modest prosperity arrived in rural areas.

The "rural paradise" was a product of industrialization. Without railways and the technology to produce mineral fertilizers, the country idyll would not have survived. But many people did not see this connection. They saw "technology" as a threat to "country nature". The small parcels of the agrarian landscape, with its hedges, pastures, meadows, and heath lands was perceived as something that needed to be protected from the "wheels of industrial progress". Such attitudes were the ideological nucleus of the nature conservation movement.

Conservation or development? Landscapes in Europe

As a general rule, we should protect and preserve those landscapes that make up Europe's character: the agrarian landscapes that evolved over hundreds and thousands of years, that contain villages and individual farms, castles set in parklands, landscape gardens and cities. In England, legislators considered such landscapes their national heritage and developed an interesting and exemplary model for the integrated conservation of rural areas. In Germany, people want to protect "nature" and created a lot of problems and misunderstandings. The landscapes created by agriculture were no longer "natural". But left to nature's devices, these cultivated lands would lose their unique character. Little by little, forests would return and cover large tracts of land, recreating the uniformity and monotony of ancient times. The diversity of European landscapes, which makes the continent so attractive and distinguishable from other parts of the world, would be lost if left to natural processes.

However, the diversity of agrarian landscapes is also put at risk by the use of large mechanical equipment for working the soil. The rural regions of one country come to resemble one another, a wheat field in Sweden is indistinguishable from a wheat field in the Po Valley or the Ukraine. For farmers, this may signify progress, but the unmistakable face of a landscape is lost in the process.

How do we protect the habitats of a broad variety of plant and animal species in the landscapes that have been created by culture? How do we integrate natural succession and change into these landscapes? These are complex problems that cannot be approached with the lachrymosity of Epimetheus. The history of the cultural landscape teaches us that there are always new "initials" for the emergence of landscape structures. With the creation of fields, railway tracks, waste dumps and parks, people also created new habitats for plants and animals, thus expanding a region's ecological diversity. In the light of such developments, opposition to the introduction of new elements into a landscape does not always make sense. Or to formulate it more provocatively: In view of the cultural landscape's historical development, we have no reason to fight the construction of golf courses or high-speed trains like the Transrapid – there is no telling today how these modern landscape elements may foster new habitats. Knowledge about the history of landscapes and the desire to understand the interaction of all the elements at play in the creation of new habitats – are important prerequisites for preserving the diversity of European landscapes. While scientific methods are important for understanding the shape of present-day landscapes, detailed historical knowledge about a landscape is necessary for the development of modern ecology, and for sensible measures to preserve nature, and state-of-the-art European landscape architecture.

Agricultural land in peri-urban areas – a plaidoyer for a palimpsest

Lionella Scazzosi

Palimpsest: this is the image which, by analogy, provides guidelines for careful and conscious reading and planning of the current characteristics of sites and of their meanings. A palimpsest is a material document that men have been writing upon, cancelling and modifying time and again, over the years. It is passed on to us, with its precious load of signs, presences and absences, all of which bear witness of these actions. Agricultural land (like all territory) is a palimpsest. It is the outcome of centuries of construction, redevelopment and maintenance in which both natural materials, such as vegetation, water, earth, stones, and artificial ones have been used. It has been intertwined with extraordinary natural events such as slides, frost, vegetal pathologies and nature's engineering with its seasonal cycles and relentless transformation of vegetable, animal and mineral matter. Sites still bear tangible marks of all the events that have occurred on them, even in those areas that are most subject to modern urbanization.

The transformations that have occurred over the last decades, following the industrialization, mechanization and rationalization of agriculture have caused the most fertile areas to be excessively exploited, a process that has involved land consolidation and homogenization, environmental decay, separation of functions and a reduction of diversity. It has also caused the most remote and peripheral areas, and those areas which are the most expensive and difficult to till (such as hilly and mountainous areas) to become abandoned or underused. In areas surrounding big cities, currently referred to as peri-urban sites and areas (zones, belts, linear conurbations etc.), limited agricultural zones can still to be found. They are often surrounded and enclosed by urban settlements, which have been studied for years and subject to specific public policies. The palimpsest here may appear impoverished, decayed, forlorn, or threatened but it has rarely been totally destroyed or replaced by a completely new landscape. Even though on a large scale, the sites appear as homogeneous areas with absolutely modern characteristics, with some observation, different signs from the past can be detected, even if they are not readily visible at first glance.

The changing fuction of agricultural land

Agriculture has always been closely linked to the town: since ancient times agricultural activities have always been linked with the town's life and they have always been carried out on the outskirts of urban settlements. Agriculture and agricultural land in today's "peri-urban" areas have quite different features, raise totally different problems and require quite different solutions. Such areas are in a very different situation compared to areas that are farther away, and more independent of, towns. They have gradually lost their historical function as areas supplying the local market; they are subject to much stronger land pressures and their functional unity is threatened by the introduction of street and power infra-structures, by manufacturing and commercial

installations, and residential settlements: all of which are the products of specific planning policies. The productive structure of these areas is often undermined for instance, through blockages of the field irrigation network in areas that long relied on such structures (e.g. the Padana and Dutch plains). They are also experiencing an abandonment of both rural buildings and agricultural activities, especially in areas where urbanization is creeping in from all sides, and where residential development is transforming and homogenizing areas that were once architecturally and agriculturally distinct. Moreover, the characteristics of agricultural society also change as, in peri-urban areas, farmers have become merely citizens whose job is farming, whereas rural areas, and particularly difficult and remote areas, are still inhabited by a farming society.

Experiments, studies, research and initiatives are and have been carried out in various countries that are trying to integrate agriculture in the town project, as a strong and permanent element with its own needs, demands and rights, that are as valid as other urban functions. Groups involved in such work include the recently established PURPLE network - Peri Urban Regions Platform Europe and a network of researchers in the field, called ENUPA-European Network on Urban and Peri-urban Agriculture. These groups aim to change the current unilateral all-urban viewpoint, which views agricultural land as empty space, to be used for urban sprawl, which can be deprived of any specific formal, historic and cultural characteristics that it may have and of its economic productive and social functions. Agriculture in peri-urban areas – and the landscape it helps to maintain - may instead contribute to the overall quality of sites from a number of different viewpoints: the environment, landscape, historic memory conservation, and quality of life for all sections of the population.

Thus the concept of multi-functionality is central in enlarging the role of agriculture and its spaces from mere production areas into recreational and tourist areas. Such a transformation needs to draw both on the knowledge of specific agricultural sites and of their historic-cultural characteristics, and on the understanding of the ways, expectations and problems of the agricultural activity itself under current conditions. The concept of multi-functionality also implies recognition of the farmers' important social role as stewards of the land; as custodians of the physical quality of sites, from the environmental and landscape viewpoint. Their role includes controlling and directing the changes brought about by nature, through works and precautionary measures against disruption. Their interventions include land arrangement, water monitoring, natural heritage management, enhancement of historical-cultural heritage and of the quality of landscape architecture. This range of tasks implies a need for social support, in terms of public awareness, funding and technical support.

Multifunctionality

In various parts of Europe management policies of agricultural land in peri-urban areas are being devised and tested. The area around Milan in Italy, is a quite significant example, as this practice has been greatly developed over recent decades and a large variety of experiments have been carried out. In the most highly urbanized areas north of Milan, a basically defensive policy has been implemented by local institutions for protecting some of the few remaining non-urbanized areas through the creation of over-municipal urban parks. These are areas, which overlap municipal boundaries, where agreements are reached between the authorities to protect the area against development, before any overall design or finance issues are agreed upon. Through such arrangements the Northern Park (Parco Nord), the Grugnotorto Park and the Brughiera Park have been added to larger and longer established regional parks, with more outstanding natural characteristics (such as the Groane Park

and the Lambro Valley Park). The case of the Milan Northern Park, one of these over-municipal parks is quite significant. The idea of the park was initially conceived in 1967, but it was not until 1983 that the redevelopment process started. Located on publicly owned land it was initially intended to be reforested. Over time part of it was formally laid out in the tradition of garden design. The project also involved the refurbishment of the historic buildings therein (a farmhouse and a 16th-century mansion with what remains of its garden) and redevelopment of the remaining physical, visual and symbolic connections that linked them to their agricultural historic setting. Another part of the park, which is private property, consists of agricultural land that is still in use, in which trails, rest areas and storage facilities for tools and machinery are being planned.

This change of strategy is, at least in part, related to the recently made choice of the Territorial Planning Board of the Province of Milan to introduce the concept of the "cultural park" to attach new meanings to sites and thereby enhance their attractiveness. For instance, the country house with adjoining agricultural land which was owned by the great Italian writer of the 19th century, Alessandro Manzoni, is located to the west of the Northern Park. This offers the opportunity for planning cultural trails, activities and educational tools linked with his life, his works and the places he mentioned in his novels, as well as his less famous activities as a botanist and a naturalist. Drawing out these links adds value to the farmland, and provides a great opportunity for local farmers to offer additional activities to citizens.

Such accomplishments are in the tradition of open air, eco- and other museums that are based on cultural trails that lead visitors through significant sites and which provide tools for enhancing symbolic sites that are important for the collective memory. These can include places that are linked with political and historic events or with famous persons, places exalted by writers and painters, religious places, historic streets and roads. They also draw on the long established traditions of parks set up for nature protection and recreation, including English parks or French and Italian regional parks.

Modes for an agricultural park

A completely different approach has been adopted in the Parco Sud, a large flat area of industrialized agriculture, south of Milan, within which some towns have developed. Since 1990 the area has been protected by the Region as an "agricultural park". Here the priorities are to reinforce

agricultural activities, protect or upgrade environmental and landscape quality, enhance historic-cultural heritage and encourage public use through the creation of well equipped trails. In this area agricultural and recreational activities (e.g. educational tourism linked with the production of organic food) are currently being integrated. They are however simple and sporadically organized activities that have to compete with very strong pressures for further development of the city of Milan and other neighbouring towns. As a result the agricultural fabric of the park is subject to frequent erosion and transformation and the creation of trails for public use is held back. In addition awareness amongst technicians and administrators of the landscape potentialities offered by agricultural land is not deeply rooted. This attitude in turn affects citizens' attitudes. Neither farmers nor politicians show a strong commitment to protecting the land from encroachment.

Set up in 1983, the regional Park of Montevecchia-Curone Valley is located between the urbanized areas of Milan and the Lecco. Whilst it has some peri-urban characteristics, it is further from the centre of Milan. Its hilly outline looms over the surrounding land and the historic characteristics of its agriculture, less industrialized than that of the plain. has created better conditions for agriculture to thrive and landscape and environment quality to be maintained. Here the authorities have found it easier to protect agricultural activities and upgrade the land for high quality production (organic, differentiated, specialized produce, etc. including the recovery of ancient and rare species), to enhance the historic-cultural and natural heritage, and to create varied and diversified activities that link agricultural production with tourist and recreational activities and thereby generate added value.

What is the role of the landscape architect in such contexts? As clearly shown by the Milan cases, the peri-urban territory undoubtedly requires specific understanding of the various forms of peri-urban agriculture, which takes different forms and has different aims, and of the landscapes with their specific historic and current characteristics. Moreover, it also requires assessing clearly the extent to which peri urban open spaces have been jeopardized and whether such damage, if it has occurred, can be reversed. The role of landscape architects should not be limited solely to reading and interpreting sites and to landscape planning, based around biological and environmental criteria balanced by the protection of historic-cultural heritage and the sites' identity. It must incorporate a wider range of perspectives and (specialized) skills. These will include economic and agronomic aspects, social ones, those wich are associated with urbanization and those which are able to tap into the potential of

agri-cultural tourism. Such tourism needs to be coupled with longer-established patterns of tourism, but relate more specifically to historic and cultural heritage. It is also extremely important to understand citizens' viewpoints more deeply, in all their varied socio-cultural aspects: their expectations of agricultural landscapes, and the cultural "lenses" through which they look at them. This in turn implies an understanding of history as such perceptions are often deeply rooted in the past. They include an idealization of nature and a search for genuinely natural sites, a defence of all forms of "biological" agriculture, a search for landscape qualities and elements typical of the past (such as Arcadia, the picturesque etc.) coupled with a difficulty in understanding the characteristics of modern-day agriculture.

On the other hand, it is also necessary to understand the farmers' viewpoints about specific real situations. These may relate to the land, to

economic, social or technical-productive restraints, as well as to family ties and specific development and enhancement potentialities.

A comprehensive approach to agricultural landscape is therefore required that is willing to accept and direct the inevitability of the processes of transformation because transformation is the main characteristic of this type of landscape. This approach will enhance the authenticity of agricultural spaces built by contemporary agriculture in its multifacetted aspects. At the same time it implies a respect for material and immaterial signs of the past and makes clear that a proper and sensible (not only compatible) contemporary project can maintain or draw out the specific landscape qualities of sites. This approach should be adopted in preference to current demands and temptations to devise idealized agrarian landscapes as, for example adopted by the French Association AMAP (Association pour le Maintien d'une Agriculture Paysanne, which aims at creating a rural society and landscape in which both inhabitants and farmers participate). Reforestation or water and wetland re-naturalization projects often do not consider the other signs of the sites' palimpsest but seek instead to wipe out time and reconstruct (although this is both impossible and anti-historical) a "natural", "original" condition.

A combined action of men and nature

The knowledge of sites is basic to any management policy that seeks to be aware of transformations. The European Landscape Convention (Florence 2000) clearly states that is particularly relevant in fast-changing areas, such as peri-urban ones. This Convention now forms a basic reference that has led to the introduction, over the last few years, of

many important new concepts and tools into the landscape culture and policy in most European countries, this despite widely different cultural, political and administrative traditions. It is not enough to make urban and rural populations understand the historic, cultural and architectural meanings that agriculture, and the landscapes it produces, have. It is not enough for them to participate in the interpretations and choices. Support for peri-urban agriculture needs to involve more than simply grafting new economic opportunities onto it. Rather it is a complex process which also involves farmers rediscovering their cultural identity and their social role, and asserting their sense of belonging to a particular place, as a counterbalance to the standardizing process of urbanization.
The rural landscape may be seen as a huge and complex historic artifact, the outcome of the combined action of men and nature throughout centuries, as a document rich in material and immaterial

signs of humanity's and nature's history. Yet it is an ever-changing and living document, rich in remnants from many ages, not just from a single epoch. It is a vast archive that enables people to know their culture, the techniques and lifestyles, as well as the nature, climate and vegetation of the past. It is an open work, where the signs of the past are intertwined with the ones that the present is leaving, continuously altering it. In a period of great transformations in the land, economy, culture and politics, such as the one we currently live in, it provides an awareness of and link with the past. It is a mirror where people may look for their identity and specificity.

Either/or, less and more – an exchange of ideas and forms

Malene Hauxner

We live in a constantly changing landscape. It is not only its use that changes, but its significance also changes. As an architectural language, landscape architecture says something about a significance that is not random and individual, but a part of the culture of the society. Because of its societal nature, its historicity and its solutions to the problems of the time, landscape architecture is not only connected to place, but also to particular epochs. The use of an architectural language is bound up with existential interpretations and the formation of semantics in a process of societal change. It is the subject of a continuous discussion of interpretation. The questions I have posed to modern landscape architecture are: whether the beautiful and true lies in what people have added or created, or in an inner order; whether this is assigned to nature or inherent forces; whether the beautiful and true in the light of contemporary demands for experience and identity lie in the abundant, pluralistic, complex and polychrome or in the small, minimal, monotone and monochrome. These two approaches, less and more, seem to be in play today, whereas in the last century it was either/or.

The modernist icons of the 20th century

An icon is not just a picture that resembles what it refers to. It is also an ideal. Understood in this way every epoch has its icons. Every epoch begins with a storm of images. The 20th century began with an image storm that approached hurricane strength. This was to the detriment of the prim, elaborate Victorian garden that the landscape garden had become, and of the architectural garden that was otherwise considered to be modern. At first the replacement icon for a small group was an avant-garde, constructivist form. In the long run, none of these images was able to provide a tool for understanding the need of the inter-war period for a tolerant attitude towards the primordial and child-like as expressed in reform and democracy movements, modern education, dance and music and the admiration for the self-sown, natural and primordial. The landscape architecture of the inter-war period was self-regulating, apparently created by nature, formulated in a language that was the result of a pastoral form of cultivation. It was to G.N. Brandt's credit that he saw that the classical pastoral landscape garden could be used in the service of the modern garden. Under Nazism and in the Second World War, enthusiasm for nature was extreme. The naked body, the woman, the native plants and untouched landscape were placed on a pedestal and any trace of the human hand was considered vandalism that left the landscape a cultural desert. The language came to expression in "Greater Copenhagen's Green Areas", in parks in the so-called "Stockholm tradition" with its legendary collaboration with nature where human intervention was invisible, and in Mariebjerg Cemetery, Aarhus University Campus, the Woodland Cemetery and the German motorways. The theory is expounded in *Gardens in the Modern Landscape* (Tunnard 1938) and *Modern* (Shepheard 1953) and in countless writings of Le Corbusier and Jens Jenson.

After the fall of Nazism and the end of the World War, one was left with the painful experience that human nature was unreliable and dangerous if it were let loose. After the Allied decision to build new welfare democracies with people at the centre, the solution had to be to educate and control human nature. In the early coldwar period it was decided that man should conquer his nature, instincts and savagery, keeping a distance from nature. The cultivated, manufactured and man-made became what was natural and thus true and beautiful. In the 1930s you were supposed to cycle into the countryside two by two or in groups and throw yourself on the grass or in the waves at the seaside. In the 1960s you flew kites, went sledging and skiing, made bonfires and put on plays. With the expulsion of parks, gardens and plants from the city, the surrounding nature became more important, and with the post-war optimistic attitude a man-made, artificial nature became a necessity. Recreational landscape was born. Whereas the ideal previously came from the pastoral landscape, it was now sought where the hand of man was most apparent, in the earth and plant-works of the agricultural landscape and in the orange groves and terraced landscapes of the South. Gardens became boxes with pebble bases and free-standing "Spanish walls" or free "rooms" made of earth and plant-works. Among the most beautiful and important are the Aabenraa mill stream and poplar avenue, Hoganas Town Hall Square, the Sculpture Garden of Neue Nationalgalerie, and outside Europe, the Sculpture Garden at the Museum of Modern Art, the Miller Garden, Paley Park and Plaza Fuente del Bebero. The theories have been formulated in articles by James C. Rose and in *Landscape for Living* (Eckbo 1950), and in *Modern Gardens and the Landscape* (Kassler 1964).

The clash with the icons of Modernism in the coldwar period

In 1968 the students demanded power to the imagination. Both American apolitical Hippies and Neo-marxists and Anarchists in France, Holland and Germany had an ingrained belief in a spontaneous, free life-style and wanted to return to nature, i.e. reconstruct and recover the natural life in all its purity and authenticity. They were supported in these ideas by the American thinker and biologist Rachel Carson who in *Silent Spring* (1963) movingly described a town where people, cattle and birds fell ill and died and a strange silence descended due to chemical pollution of the air, water and earth. If birds and insects were important for the survival of humanity, then spraying, clipping and pruning of their life support would be catastrophic and flowers and fruit should be left and the grass allowed to grow tall. The conclusion must be that bio-diversity was beautiful. This new knowledge influenced iconography and architecture. The Dutch artist Louis Le Roy wrote *"Natuur uitschakelen: natuur inschakelen"* which title implies that man has mistakenly seen nature as a machine that could be switched on and off. Roy's theory of "the art of cultivation" became the basis of an aesthetic that distanced itself from the picture of the

beautiful as a result of human intervention In addition, there was an idea
that it was meaningless to recreate a particular lost landscape, to stylize
the cultural landscape, as had been good practice in the previous decade.
On the small scale, these theories resulted in the closely-cut grass being
allowed to grow long, and weeds being allowed to grow in the beds.
On the large scale, it resulted in "nature in the city", at the same time
as the focus moved from the city, and garden art towards the open
countryside and environmental projects.
A mainstream perception is that Holland swears by the man-made
language and that this is because the Dutch have always had to wrest the
land from the sea. This has at times resulted in precisely the apparently
natural becoming the icon. It was in Holland that the German concept of
heempark developed and it was in the Bijlmermeer development in
Amsterdam that the pastoral landscape of *Ville Radieuse* was carried out.

In Sweden the regional, nature-conserving ideal had been prominent in
the urban landscape since the 1920s. Archipelago and leafy meadow,
the right to roam and the democratic, relaxed life-style entered into such
a close symbiosis that the language up to the present has the status
of the natural and true. In Denmark C.Th. Sørensen had held his own
against naturalism, but when motorway planning started seriously in the
1970's, it was the 1930s icon, not that of the 1950s that was used. It
was Alwin Seifert's reprint of articles from the 1930s that made it a duty
to avoid non-indigenous plants.
After the youth and student protests that had taken on the character of
a cultural revolution, the focus shifted from the cultivated, man-made
landscape, from the powerful avenues and sharp woodland fringes of the
country house estate to the leafy meadows and flowery fields of the small
farmstead. From now on, the hand of nature dominated the architectural

language in those gardens that had become free areas. The quality increased proportionally to the lack of human effort. Through diversity and great species variety, nature could adjust itself to changing conditions. Arguments could be found here for the battle against monoculture that was also taking place in the architectural discourse, in *A Pattern Language* (Christopher Alexander, 1977).

Enthusiasm for nature went hand in hand with a goodbye to expertise, the elite and the role of the heroic architect. Architects came down to earth and explored nature to find structures. Only complex structures could excite, as followed from *Complexity and Contradiction in Architecture* (Venturi, 1966) and *Learning from Las Vegas* (Venturi, Scott Brown et al., 1972. Ian McHarg thought that if the process was correct, good form would follow (*Design with Nature*, 1969).

French landscape architecture shows its strength in the forms: from Renaissance and Baroque gardens to Parisian boulevards flanked by promenade parks in the 1850-1870s - "le genre mixte". However, Gilles Clément should not be forgotten, who in 1978 tentatively began to remove non-indigenous plants from his garden and to prune trees and shrubs as if they stood in a leafy meadow. Nor for the "stray plants" and the "garden in motion" he later introduced into public space. The taste for the self-setting, redundant, neglected and ruined areas, the wasteland of which there was more and more with the decline of industry, was reflected by the American artist Robert Smithson. Interest was directed towards the forces and processes of nature that replaced images of nature. The different states of water, from steam to ice, were experimented with in a new aesthetic that created a newly discovered form for the iconic landscape. With new computer techniques, it became

possible to let water spring. Innumerable plazas and parks benefited from this technique. In this period Europe looked to the USA, to landscapes by Peter Walker, Georges Hargreaves and Michael van Valkenburg. Martha Schwartz's use of pop and bagels, sweets and gilded frogs of everyday culture was not emulated by European landscape architects. But the syntax was. The rotated, superimposed grid became an accepted part of the post-modern landscape-architectural language.

In the 1980s the floodgates were opened and the city was invaded by the 1960s enemy, nature, that had now become a friend everyone paid court to. Facades became green and grass was allowed to cover roofs, garden rubbish was composted, shrubs and trees with edible berries were planted, the sun's rays and rainwater were collected and recycled. The 1980s was a decade where everything should be made visible,

both history and the ecological cycle. Bernard Huet revealed historic structures in squares and parks in Paris. Bernhard Korte recreated the delta landscape of the Rhineland from the Napoleonic period and Bernard Lassus integrated several historical layers in Rochefort-sur-Mer and created a connection between park and city that made history and place understandable and authentic.

In his thesis on the Berlin Wall, Rem Koolhaas presented us with an idea of architecture as landscape. After the wall fell, the question of cultural identity was pressing. In the landscape park of Duisburg Nord designed by Peter Latz, nature and culture were turned upside down or plaited together in a remembrance landscape of working class culture with coalmines which had now been rediscovered as the basis of modern society and the prosperity of the German working classes.

With the optimistic post-war attitude, a man-made, artificial nature became a necessity:
C. Th. Sørensen's Aabenraa Millstream and Poplar Avenue, Denmark 1950.

Parks are composed of contrasting layers from the 1980s on: The Scent Garden in
Ronneby Brunns Park, Sweden, by Sven Ingvar Andersson.

Another aspect of Ronneby Brunns Park: the Japanese Garden.

Since the 1980s, attention has been directed towards place, its character, individuality or spirit. The concept *Genius Loci* put forward by the Norwegian architecture theoretician Christian Norberg-Schultz had the aim of making architecture original and rooted. This paradigm has had a decisive influence on present-day landscape architecture with a tendency to be elevated into law. It was Rem Koolhaas who first questioned its validity in his article, "The Generic City".

Aldo Rossi's *Una Analoga Citta*, a fictive city in a North Italian landscape and Paolo Portoghesi's *Strada Novissima* at the Vienna Biennial made way for the free choice of post-modernism in the historical archive. At the IBA exhibition in Berlin, European Neo-rationalism and American Post-modernism were blended, just as classical housing blocks with courtyards and green façades were combined with recycling of waste water and

greenhouses on the roofs. The classical language of architecture was reborn in Rob and Leon Krier's neo-traditional building plans. As in early Classicism, a formal classical architectural language was combined with a pastoral language in landscape architecture. In Leon Krier's proposal for *Quartier de la Villette*, ruinous dilapidated street-trees grew among pillars and pediments and in the parks there were water-holes that only lacked the grazing animals to form a perfect pastoral idyll. In Scandinavia the result was not ecological exploitation of roofs, façades and rubbish, but lots of nature in the form of plants. In the 1980s the park reappeared and Sven-Ingvar Andersson contributed, with due acknowledgement of C.Th. Sørensen's book *Parkpolitik i Sogn og Kobstad* (Park Policy in Parish and Town, 1931), to the reintroduction of the park policy concept. The regeneration of Les Halles in Paris led away from the nature-like with trellises in typical 1880s style. But it was only after the big competition

for Parc de la Villette (1982) that it was clear that the icon had changed. The programme required a culture park with activities, a wood consisting not of trees, but of social arrangements. Bernard Tschumi's park with a theoretical background in Jacques Derrida's and Peter Eisenman's deconstructionism was of international importance. The same applied to the other first-prize winning proposals by Rem Koolhaas, Andreu Arriola, Alexandre Chemetoff, Gilles Vexlard and Sven-Ingvar Andersson, whose proposal was called particularly Scandinavian.

The icon associated with the resulting "park-mania" made use of neither "more" nor "less", but of "both / and" composed of contrasting layers, stripes and stacks. The contrasting pairs were the artificial contra the natural, the clear contra the opaque, the urban contra the rural. The grid and "the waving line of beauty" were compressed to symbolise

Nietzsche's principles of art, the Apollonian and the Dionysian. It is a language one can study in Ayala Park in Manila, Parc du Sausset in France, Fatburpark, in the competition proposals for the park of the 21st century, in the two gardens at the Nordform Exhibition, in the scented garden and the Japanese garden in Ronneby Brunnspark in Sweden and in the proposals for Hedehusene Park in Denmark

The real focus became Barcelona, which like the rest of Spain had received a new democratic constitution in 1978. The parks acquired components such as lakes with rowing boats, grassy slopes with running tracks and ruin fragments with waterfalls that provided decoration, activity and story-telling. On centre-stage came play with natural and artistic things of beauty as expressed in the Parc Joan Miró and the garden at Villa Cecilia. Barcelona continued its success and renewed its language

with new icons, told new stories with other meanings: the Parc de la Trinitat, Jardin Botanic, Passeig Maritim de la Barceloneta and the new folded landscapes in Barcelona's mountainous suburbs.

Into the complex society of the 21st century

In the 1990s a picture takes shape of a greater belief in the future, in the ability of people to solve problems with the aid of knowledge and technology. People are no longer paralysed with fears of overpopulation, atomic warfare and pollution and have not yet been terrified by terrorism and fundamentalism. The landscape-architectural icon shows a new, logical, pragmatic objectivity, with emphasis on the regulative aspect, like that of the post-war period but with a new insight into the processes of nature. The man-made has regained its position as beautiful and true,

especially in continental landscape architecture. Inspiration comes from cultivating plants, and an admiration for earthworks and the cultural and ecological cycles. A new French wave appears with the students from Ecole Nationale Supérieure du Paysage de Versailles. Perhaps it began with the two special gardens in Parc de la Villette; Jardin des Bambous and Jardin de la Treille, which pushed into prominence the mileposts of French culture, the kitchen and the garden.

The trend became clearer at Place de la Bourse in Lyon, in Desvigne's and Dalnoky's factory in Guyancourt and Agence Ter's High School in Nîmes. Yves Brunier showed particular interest in cultivation in his models and colourful sketches. The desire to move up into the light was strong. Whilst previously it was thought people should walk in the shade of the luxuriant trees now they should climb onto bridges and decking to look out over gardens, plains and water. The elements of the city such as

airport lights and runways, the asphalt and barriers of the motorways take their place on an equal footing with the landscape and the art of cultivation.

The focus has shifted from the cultural landscape of the French suburbs and the mountain slopes of the Catalan suburbs towards cities and ports. The crucible is Rotterdam and the alchemists OMA, MVRDV and West 8. The theory can be studied in SMLXL, FARMAX, and in *In Holland staat een huis*, the catalogue for the exhibition at NAI, Rotterdam 1995. Poetry and technology are united in striped and stacked landscapes that need not be catalogued under architecture, town planning, landscape architecture or garden art. The identity is not in the place but is created by virtue of what it is to be human. The 1990s icon Schouwburgplein is composed of an abundance of materials in a rectangular, orthogonal syntax. But no sooner

has an icon impressed itself on our consciousness than a new one jumps out, this time a biomorphic language without Euclidian geometry without hierarchy, without straight lines, in a flowing composition of spaces, as the last two *Topos European Landscape Award winners*, Stig L. Andersson and Karres en Brands, have documented.

Society appears today as a complex society with the fundamental characteristic that it can also be different. Whilst previously the landscape's function was movement and sojourn, it is today identity and adventure and for this neither the image of the pastoral landscape nor the agricultural landscape is enough. Now biotechnological, cultural and natural history processes are required. Experiences of contingency, the idea that something can always be different, perhaps lead to this amorphous language that seems as though it could change shape

◂◂ The deconstructivist principle characterizes the Barcelona parks of the 1980s and 1990s:
Villa Cecilia Park by Elias Torres Tur and José Antonio Martínez Lapeña, Barcelona 1981.
◂ Villa Cecilia Park.
▾ Carlos Ferrater's and Bet Figueras' Botanical Garden, Barcelona 1999.

at any moment. With the development of the language of contingency and icons of contingency, it will perhaps become possible to deal with the cornucopia of possibilities in the complex society. In Copenhagen the pillars of the new theatre will be sloping, like those of the iconic station square in Barcelona, at Villa Dall'Ava and in the secret Mikado Garden at the Bo01 Exhibition in Malmö. One could be forgiven for thinking that this is the same playing with nature that Alvar Aalto used many years ago when he gave pillars the shape of forest tree-trunks. Perhaps this is just an expression of the amorphous nature of everything, and of the fact that not even pillars can be fixed.

In these times with national canons, I find it fascinating that iconography can wander, if not globally, at least from one end of Europe to the other; that the Catalonian architect Enric Miralles could be inspired by the

Norwegian architect Sverre Fehn's ideas about movement, when he created the Igualada Cemetery, a work so unique that it has never been translated.

Central Europe, a moving playing field

Gertjan Jobse

Landscape architecture in Central Europe is developing quickly but is not without problems. What do we know about the state of the profession and education in the Czech and Slovak Republics, Poland and Hungary? Where do landscape architects work and what do they think? What makes Central Europe so fascinating? It is an area where landscape architecture has experienced a turbulent development in recent years and is gaining growing self-confidence. Still, a lot of questions remain for the future: on professional rights, the improvement of quality and on how education and research will develop in the new Europe.

Calling the heart of Europe "East" or "Ost" is wrong. Since the political division of Europe is over, this term is considered pejorative. Hungarians, Poles, Slovakians and Czech prefer to see themselves as Central Europeans. As Balázs Almási from Hungary comments diplomatically, "Let's hope it's just a small clerical error".

The history of landscape architecture in Central Europe before 1939 is similar to elsewhere in Europe. The landscape design tradition dates from 1853 when formal horticultural training began in Budapest. Moreover, there are many showpieces of romantic park design. For example, the parks Łazienki in Warsaw, Lednice-Valtice in the Czech Republic and the landscape gardens of Furst Pückler in Muskau, straddling the Polish-German border. Often foreign landscape architects, working peripatetically, designed these places. In 1814 the "father of the modern suburb" British landscape designer John Claudius Loudon toured Central Europe. His Grand Tour taught him to see landscape "less as a frame for a variety of aesthetical experiences, but more as the territory of a new social order" (Sudjic, 1992).

Pioneers

The 1920s and 1930s saw the rise of an avant-garde: "Individuals who more or less by their self-education and practice gained good knowledge and experience" says Honza Jokl of the Czech Republic. Unfortunately, the postwar division of Europe interrupted these developments. Jokl describes how "the Communists definitely did not encourage landscape architecture, so we were stuck to our glorious past from Renaissance and Baroque times". Moreover, the coming of the Iron Curtain cut off landscape architects from colleagues elsewhere. This closed environment caused a serious set back, for cultural bridges between East and West. Professor Alina Drapella-Hermansdorfer from Wroclaw describes the post war scene thus: "Under the pressure of immediate needs, there was no demand for new design solutions; so the profession focused on conservation and reconstruction."

Despite successful city reconstruction projects after the Second World War, landscape architecture was not fully acknowledged. Modernist, system-built, apartment blocks were set in uniform and functional green areas (Gal, 2001). These spaces are not especially exciting, though they may offer comfortable living space.

However, Central European universities were pioneers in laying the foundations for landscape planning and protection. Schools for landscape design were established in Poland (Warsaw, 1948), Hungary (Corvinus University, 1963), and at the Slovak Academy of Sciences (Bratislava, 1970). Based on landscape ecology principles, their approach developed integrated methods for land evaluation and planning. This led to the establishment of national and landscape parks and the successful application of landscape zoning in large agglomerations.

Only after the 1989 fall of the Berlin Wall, did outdoor design in cities start to play an important role again. The seeds for this were developed in the academies in the previous decades as a critique of modernism. Honza Jokl describes the changes in the Czech Republic: "The country opened up and we started to see the world had moved since 1968. It was a shock and until now the profession has not regained its full respect."

Mental landscapes

The challenges are enormous, but are landscape architects prepared? What do landscape architects in Central Europe think? Is their "mental landscape" different than those in the rest of Europe? Outsiders often think that the mind of the *Homo sovieticus* is still overpowering, but probably the opposite is true. Central Europe has become a bridge again and Central Europeans are eager to find connections with the rest of Europe. We can see this in the involvement of individuals in international organizations like EFLA, IFLA and ELASA, as well as in practice and academic thinking.

Two strains of thought in contemporary landscape design can be distinguished. Alina Drapella-Hermansdorfer describes one of them thus: "The first is highly advanced and oriented towards management and preservation of natural and cultural heritage and its most distinctive features." As taught at the agricultural universities, this approach has close links to land use and natural sciences. It played an important role in spatial policies, but has to generate new models for viable landscape design.

The other approach concentrates on urban questions as Bernadett Jobbágy from Hungary observes: "All around Europe landscape architecture is changing, the question is how to consciously apply principles of sustainability into practice: to our daily life in cities." Initially this second line of thought "combines standards of sustainable planning, technology and architecture in the design of urban places" (Alina Drapella-Hermansdorfer). Taught at the technical universities, this approach has a big future with more urban expansions and revitalization planned.

Public notions

However clear this theoretical distinction may be, public notions about space and landscape vary greatly. When asked what binds the countries of Central Europe, people sceptically reply it is the common lack of appreciation for landscape and public space. Professor Aleksander Böhm from Kraków explains: "Communal space belonged to nobody, so in general people have a low appreciation of public spaces: they are neglected and increasingly become privatised." Consequently, more and more "substitutes" are created, which are carefully designed places with restricted access. Traditional, communally used public space disappears as the focus "on economic forces considers greenery as peripheral" notes Agnieszka Paderewska. Dömötör Tamás from Hungary adds that since the "big boom" in the 90s, there has been a recent slow down. "There are bigger projects in the capital, but developers save money on green spaces."

But there is good news, after the rapid initial influx of foreign investment, the situation is now changing and appropriate design becomes more appreciated. Aleksander Böhm comments: "With new lifestyles and better living conditions, the identity of space is regarded as having a market value: beauty pays. The public needs improvement and there is a growing demand for the design of squares and other spaces. Consequently our position in urban planning is changing."

Peter Gal notes that the same is happening in the Slovak Republic, with innovative design projects and planning approaches. Outdoor space and landscape increases in importance and possibilities for landscape architects are expanding at all levels, from spatial planning to private gardens. The situation is less buoyant in the Czech Republic, as Honza Jokl says: "The feeling for cityscapes within society is pretty low, but the

identification and sensitiveness towards the Czech landscape is much greater. Maybe, Czech society is still searching for its attitude towards the city."

Fresh diplomacy

Is the life of our Central European colleagues so different? Probably not: they are as busy and ambitious as elsewhere. Work and life seem to be more interwoven, but this might be because earnings in Central Europe are far lower and people simply have to work more. Flóra Möcsényi from Budapest notes: "Nowadays you can live a normal life, but you have to work hard for it." Bernadett Jobbágy describes an ordinary day at work in Hungary: "They get up, drink coffee, work all day and in a lucky case finish at 5 pm or chase new jobs and teach and publish." Polish Dorota

Rudawa explains that running her office, securing contracts and talking to clients comes first and absorbs more than half of her time, leaving less for concept design and quality checks.

But the status of landscape architects in society is different from Western Europe. The general public often has little idea of what landscape architects do, or sees them as gardeners. Flóra Möcsényi notes that "generally people on the streets have never heard of our profession". "They are surprised and shout: what a nice job!" says Balázs Almási "but they actually know nothing about it". His colleague Bernadett Jobbágy thinks it all depends upon landscape architects' visibility: "Society should say what it expects of us, but we ourselves don't know our tasks and what we are capable of yet."

At the same time landscape architects have an important role to play in regaining the public realm. By demonstrating the attractiveness of public

places they can make society more sensitive towards landscape. Katarina Urbanska thinks more promotion is needed in Slovakia: "Landscape architects just need to go out, show up and appear to the world."
As professionals, they have skills to express ideas graphically and implement them technically. Along with creativity and technical know-how, diplomacy and presentation are crucial in convincing people of their environmental choices. No other profession knows how to deal with changes over time and carry out comprehensive planning in such width and depth. This is the role landscape architects can play throughout Central Europe. Collaboration with architects and other disciplines is required as interests converge. Students of ELASA stress that the professional basis should be strong: "If the centre is empty, our profession will be an air balloon and anybody can play with it." (Jobbágy, 2004).

Superfluous

Paradoxically, many landscape architects find employment in garden design. The number of purely landscape architectural offices is still low; only Hungary has more than fifty. Most landscape architects are one person practices or freelancers; in all four countries, a few larger offices co-exist with many small ones. Joanna Milewska notes another pattern: "Often people with ideas brought these from abroad. In the academies, a lack of international literature makes it difficult to prepare a new generation."
A lack of jobs and internships forces students to go abroad, but once they come back they carry a load of experiences and contacts with them. Multi-disciplinary offices with architects and engineers are common in Hungary, the Czech and Slovak Republics. These evolved from pure architectural practices and some former State Planning Offices (Jámbor, 2001). Dorota Rudawa notes that in Poland "pure" landscape design

The artificial palm tree located in the middle of Rondo De Gaulle in Warsaw and designed by Joanna Rajkowska is an essential landmark in the city ("palma" means "unthinkable" in Polish).

The central garden of MOM Park in Budapest. This large residential estate, shopping and entertainment centre is an example of new commercial architecture in Hungary. (Photo: Aniko Andor)

In workshops across Central Europe, students explore new design ways and discover unknown sources of inspiration. These "free thinking" exercises result in experiments and concepts, like the "breads on the land" in Kapolcs in Hungary. (Photo: Joanna Milewska)

Slovakian mountain landscape. (Photo: Ladislav Bakay)

offices hardly exist: "Most freelancers not only design, but also build gardens, as clients are not prepared to pay for something as superfluous as a plan."

Important for the development and emancipation of the profession is professional control. Ideally such appreciation comes through a recognised title, protected by an architectural chamber. "Basically anybody can do greenery without any restrictions" says Joanna Milewska. While landscape architects can register in architectural chambers in the Czech Republic and Hungary, their Polish colleagues are still fighting to get official recognition of their professional status.

In a large country such as Poland, the combination of a closed circle of architects and a low level of organization of landscape architects themselves worsens this situation. Different schools do collaborate, but at present no nationwide landscape architectural union exists.

In the Slovak Republic, the situation is different again, as the architects' chamber supports landscape architects and recently introduced legislation allowing access after a few years of practice.

Perhaps the best situation exists in Hungary, where magazines and landscape architectural organizations provide the necessary platform for exchange and information. Still, competition between rival organizations may paralyse the profession as a whole. The majority of the landscape architects are Budapest based, the eastern part and the countryside are left deserted.

Outstanding projects

What do landscape architects work on? Slovakian Maria Bihunova says: "Basically all fields are covered: design of open and communal spaces

59

like streets, squares parks and green areas, cemeteries, sport grounds and more recently also inner yards of offices, shopping centres, recreational areas, etc." "Site design is indeed the most common task", adds Peter Gabor "but regulation and rehabilitation plans and studies or impact assessments are carried out as well".
Recently, there has been a growth of city parks and many are being conserved on a historical basis. Most new parks are either privately financed or developed as prestigious municipal projects, like the roof park on the Library of Warsaw University and the Millennium Park in Budapest. This former Ganz Factory has been reconstructed into a modern, city centre urban park of 35,000 square metres.

There are a number of successful projects on a regional scale, such as nature conservation projects. The riverside restoration project in the

Green Islands Programme in Wroclaw combines water management, housing and recreation in an attractive and sustainable urban plan. Impressive results have been achieved in Hungary. At the beginning of the 1980s the water quality of Lake Balaton (the biggest sweet water lake in Europe) declined, due to run-off of agricultural chemicals and draining of swamps. A wetland was reconstructed and since 1992 this has functioned as a filter. The water quality improves year by year and many rare bird species have returned. This experience can be used for rehabilitation projects: of other wetlands, as well as of heavily polluted, former industrial areas.

With the coming of foreign investment and the growth of middle-class demand, the budgets for commercial projects have grown. This has led to landscape architects designing the external spaces of new shopping

Elizabeth Square in Budapest (2002), with a cultural centre under the park. The square is designed by Zsuzsanna Bogner, Péter Balogh and Tamás Sándor.

centres, like the Gallery Mokotów in Warsaw (2000), which was very simple in treatment. More recent and exciting examples elsewhere include the terraces, bridge and green roof of the Nový Smíchov shopping centre and the adjacent Sacré Coeur Hill in Prague (see page 214). Miasteczko Wilanów in Warsaw is an example of a public space with attractive housing. The plan is coherent and, according to the French chief architect Guy Perry, the spaces between the three-to-five-story buildings will be as important as the buildings themselves.

Dreams and perspectives

What does the future bring? What are the major challenges for the future? We can conclude that the profession in Central Europe is reclaiming its position and in the words of Balázs Almási is "on the way towards a big future". Katarina Urbanska adds: "There is plenty of potential for development, restructuring and restoration."

The accession of the central European countries to the European Union marks the era of a new age. No longer separate, collaboration and exchange across the wider Europe becomes more possible. The academic world proceeds with common exchange projects and the first steps for a European graduate programme, but there is still a lack of accessible information. We must dare to "learn from the mistakes and successes of others and share our global experience in Europe" says Guy Perry. "To avoid making costly mistakes, a profoundly contextual approach to shaping the environment is needed."

Another important success factor is whether landscape architecture can promote itself in society, influence attitudes towards landscape and collaborate with other design disciplines. With the improving economy and

61

standard of living, the appreciation of public space is increasing. In order to achieve recognition it is important that the profession organizes itself better, solves internal difficulties and establishes professional standards and legislation.

Increasing privatization and a lack of public projects cause an unstable market and a strong dependence on private clients. The difficult situation of physical planning and turbulent market forces make adjustment and flexibility a basic necessity. In such a setting, those who manage to survive and experiment are really good. "Competition is perhaps not bad for the level and quality of the work", says Bernadett Jobbágy. „The question is 'to save a bit of an architectural idea'", concludes Dorota Rudawa. Alina Drapella-Hermansdorfer is more critical: "When the mark of social success and prestige is by having plants and building

material looking just like the illustrated journals, these developers lead a drive to unify standards." As Agnieszka Paderewska comments on the situation in Poland: "We just need some time to improve existing structures and prepare the ground for new changes", Joanna M lewska adds: "It is now up to young, talented designers to come up with innovative ideas." This young, mobile generation has the energy for change. "We have to keep our eyes open, since it is our future and all these projects will influence our prospective work."
Ladislav Bakay believes that "he who knows what he wants and goes for it can really be a shooting star!" Innovative projects that foster creativity are just a start, but a growing reputation and recognition in society have to be earned by hard work, knowledge and a bit of craziness. In the words of Bernadett Jobbágy: "You have to be brave, but professional."

The public Millennium Park in Budapest (3.5 ha) celebrates the creation of temporal space usage. In the interactive part, mobile elements invite the visitors to create their own actual surrounding. The motivational part shows the normal environment in an unusual form. Designers: Árpád Kovács, Gábor Lendvai, Johanna Muszbek, Péter Pozsár, Dominika Tihanyi (Uj Irany Group).

The youngest geographical land in Poland, Żuławy, is also the lowest, with one third of the surface below sea level. The river Vistula enters a lagoon of the Baltic Sea through several branches, leaving layers of fertile deposit behind. The area is intersected by a network of melioration channels, which protect the polders from being flooded.

The pioneers

Karin Helms

The profession of landscape architecture in Europe is still young; at least its origins are still within living memory. In nearly all European countries we can still talk in person to the people who founded or initiated landscape architecture as a profession. Their work is just beginning to be recognized; sometimes it is even becoming part of the cultural heritage. It is important to tell the story of these living sources of European landscape, in direct conversation either with them or their closest colleagues, in order to understand the circumstances of their lives that made this emergence of landscape possible and how it was subsequently passed on to the next generation. Meeting the founders and comparing the sources of European landscape will allow us to more readily understand the abundance of the trends and the roads taken in order to be better able to continue to develop them. Almost every country in Europe recognizes one or more personalities or authors who were able to attract particular and lasting attention to the question of landscape, to found a specific school or training course and/or to promote the growth of the profession. From a long list of names, we can cite Pietro Porcinai in Italy, Brandt and Sørensen in Denmark, Hermann Mattern and Leberecht Migge in Germany, Simon and Corajoud in France… Let us start this series of encounters related to the emergence of the profession arbitrarily with two pairs: Jacques Simon and Michel Corajoud for France, and Georg Boye and Reynir Vilhalmsson for Iceland.

Michel Corajoud – learning from Jacques Simon

At the end of the 1960s, re-thinking society was a matter of urgency. It was a rich and troubled period of ferment in France after the war in Algeria with the repatriation of the French from North Africa and the rural exodus to the big cities. A cooperative of intellectuals and practitioners set up a multidisciplinary studio called AUA (Atelier d'Urbanisme et d'Architecture) to find spatial responses to contemporary questions relating to housing, the living environment and the emerging city. Jacques Simon, appointed by Paul Chemetov, one of the most prominent architects of the AUA, joined the team and immediately found himself faced with the rapid transformation of town and country and the creation of large-scale residential developments and large urban parks.

Simon, son of a nurseryman, was first trained as a reporter-photographer and then, at 30 years of age, as a horticultural engineer at the ENSH (École Nationale Supérieure d'Horticulture) in Versailles. He brought with him a different type of response to urban questions, based on a creativity that focused on living matter as the foundation of a project. It was a new design conception, far removed from the know-how at the time, when vegetation was considered more as decoration. After Versailles, Simon spent two years in Sweden, nourishing his ideas with the Scandinavian approach to public space and the subject of nature in the city. His young colleague at the AUA, Michel Corajoud, was fascinated by him: "Simon is at ease with great broad expanses, able to model a horizon with his own two hands." Simon has a physical relationship to the earth, even if it means using agricultural explosives and bulldozers in order to feel the terrain in terms of masses, to sculpt the ground, to terrace it with convex-concave relationships, sheltered or exposed, and so on. He flies over his work in a helicopter, then in a microlight aircraft, and takes photos of it – which makes him a precursor of the land-art movement.

Jacques Simon travelled a lot. "He is a photographer, globetrotter, citizen of the world: at every event, the eruption of Mount Etna, the Berlin Wall... he was there!" recalls Corajoud. Simon is in phase with the world's energy. He founded the journal Espaces verts with his photos and shock collages, his sketches and his on-the-spot reflections. The periodical was published from 1968 to 1982, with a total of 54 issues.

Corajoud, only a draughtsman at the time, was "snapped up" by Simon at the AUA. He not only was inventive but also understood the complex organization of landscape: "Simon's vision was sound, he knew how to

spot the issues at stake right away, he radiated energy and wanted to get things done." They worked together for a year and a half. The coalition of the Simon-Corajoud pair was a period of initiation for the latter. As far as pedagogy is concerned, one could say that Jacques Simon is the originator, the "starter", and Michel Corajoud is the "motor" of the development and organization of teaching landscape in France. For "Simon's speed is dazzling. The time it takes to teach is too slow for him", testifies Corajoud.

In 1971, Michel Corajoud found himself in the midst of historic circumstances that not only allowed him to join the staff at the school in Versailles, the ENSH, but also to have a free hand. "The school was in a crisis, everyone left because they said it would close. That allowed me to do what I wanted: to work on projects. Teaching was organized along the

• Jacques Simon, first trained as a photographer-reporter, than as a horticultural engineer, has a physical relat onship to the earth which fascinated his colleague Michel Corajoud. Sculpting the ground, even with explosives or bulldozers, and flying over his work in a helicopter to take pictures he is a precursor of land art.
• In 1971, Michel Corajoud succeeded a new start of the École Nationale Supérieure du Paysage in Versailles where Jacques Simon was already teaching. Corajoud introduced his students to ways of manoeuvring in and through the landscape project – Versailles is today a project-oriented school.

lines of a dual relationship instead of a group one. The teacher was there to accompany and increase the value of the student's work." Corajoud arrived with a culture of the city and of the project that was very different from Versailles and from his horticulture school. His references had developed both from having met Simon and from the culture of the AUA, which was oriented on urbanism, architecture and the idea of the suburb. Corajoud brought with him a new form of education: "The *Beaux Arts* system was buried in '68, along with its ceremonial, its theatricals around the project and its freshman initiation rituals. The question is to know how to escort the students through a project without this dramatization, with what is implemented in the project." That was what the architect Henri Ciriani, his associate in the AUA, was explaining. Corajoud tried to teach students how to manoeuvre in and through the project. He is a project-oriented pedagogue.

The key period is thus between 1971 and 1974 at Versailles, between the end of the horticulture school and the beginning of the landscape school. Michel Corajoud having arrived at the right time with the right baggage caused a new generation of landscape architects to emerge in France in record time. He is responsible not for an idea but for a dynamic that gave landscape architects an appetite for the project.

Reynir Vilhalmsson – learning from Georg Boye

It was in the post-war period that landscape architecture education became organized in Denmark, both at the Royal School of Agriculture (KVL) and the Academy of Arts (KA). In 1944, a summer seminar brought together four landscape architects: G.N. Brandt, C.Th. Sørensen, Georg Georgsen and Georg Boye, and urban planners. Their objective was to establish conditions for teaching a landscape project, including studios, theory courses and excursions. The success of this seminar, which had 50 participants in all, was the basis for the first academic programme on landscape at the KA in 1949 with Carl Theodor Sørensen as the principal teacher. Boye, who had worked for Sørensen's firm in the 1930s, was the only one of the four landscape architects who did not ultimately join that school. Instead, he devoted his efforts to the KVL, namely the horticulture and landscape section, where he completely organized landscape education, separating it clearly from horticultural training in 1960.

Boye became a professor of landscape, as did Sørensen, in 1963. Between the end of the 1940s and 1960, two educational systems for landscape at the university level were thus set up in Denmark: a première in Europe.

Rivalry between these two schools was strong and debates were intense during this "golden age" of landscape. Georg Boye, less well known than Sørensen, perhaps because he is closer to technology than the arts, was nevertheless very active in promoting the profession. From 1920 on, he devoted himself to a new landscape journal with the title of *Have arkitekten*, which tried to get away from the "art of the garden" in order to concentrate on the conception of public spaces. He was also active from 1949 to 1956 as Denmark's representative in the International Federation of Landscape Architects (IFLA).

‣ Georg Boye organized landscape education at the Copenhagen based Royal School of
Agriculture (KVL) in 1960, establishing a rivalry with the landscape programme of the Academy
of Arts (KA) headed by C.Th. Sørensen.
‣ Reynir Vilhalmsson came from Iceland to Denmark, studied and worked with Georg Boye
from 1953 to 1963 and brought back a new understanding of landscape to a country where
the winter lasts nine months. In the following years, he established the profession of
landscape architecture in Iceland.

Meeting and collaborating with Boye was decisive for Reynir Vilhalmsson and for the development of the profession of landscape architecture in Iceland. Born in 1934, Reynir was sent to Norway at 14 as a farm-hand after the early death of his father, lost at sea. There he discovered the farmlands with their ploughed fields, the fertile soil worked by human hands, the fields of grain, the rye for baking bread, and above all the vast forests. All of these things were unknown in Iceland, a country with volcanic soil, which lived basically from fishing. At 17 he returned to Iceland to be trained as a gardener at the polytechnic in Rikisins.

Encouraged by one of his teachers, Jon Björnsson, the first nurseryman and owner of a gardening business in Iceland, Reynir left for Denmark to take the first courses on garden planning. "I took a one-year course in 1953 at the KVL headed by Georg Boye. I think he was experimenting with us, trying out his educational methods, which he subsequently developed at the KVL landscape school. We were only ten students, all members of an association of landscape architects, and we were very enthusiastic about the feeling of being the pioneers of landscape."

Reynir profited from this bubbling turmoil. He attended all the lectures and seminars and followed Georg Boye in his landscape firm for several years. In parallel to working at the firm, he took courses at the KA, the school competing with the KVL, where he met Sørensen and became his student as well. "I cannot help admiring Sørensen; I think he is the only true genius I ever met. But I am profoundly grateful for the years spent with Georg Boye and for those at the firm of the couple Agnete Muusfeldt and Erik Mygind." In this "golden age" of landscape, Reynir was entirely under the influence of the Danish modern movement. He worked on many projects, one of which is very famous and was photographed by Yann Arthus Bertrand: the circular gardens in Brondby, south of Copenhagen, which were inspired by the shape of the paddocks enclosing the small Icelandic horses when they are for sale.

In 1963, having spent ten years in Denmark, Reynir returned to Iceland. "I was not sure there would be any real possibilities for a landscape architect to practise in this country where the winter lasts nine months." Reynir, the first Icelandic landscape architect, started working freelance at the age of 29. It was during the period of massive rural exile to the capital city Reykjavik. New city districts had to be built. Everything had to be invented. Well-qualified through his professional experience in Denmark, he developed numerous projects. With the realization of the Ellidaàrdalur urban development to his name, he became a combination of landscape architect and urban planner. The develpment covers 400 hectares built around the river and the forest he planted on a lava field in 1974. His former teacher, Jon Björnsson, educated at Cornell, established the Alaska Nursery, named after the trees from Alaska that he managed to acclimatize in Iceland. Such know-how allowed Reynir to realize his projects, developing "living" vegetation in a country that was not accustomed to relating to plants in this way.

The profession of landscape architecture in Iceland has developed enormously since then. There are now 50 landscape architects that are members of the federation for a population of 280,000: one of the highest percentages in Europe. In the 1980s the landscape architects started developing a specific vocabulary to stage the characteristic Icelandic climatic and geological features and materials such as lava in their urban projects. They also work on more large-scale problems now, even on a territorial scale. Here again Reynir Vilhjalmsson served as an example when he set up an anti-avalanche wall in Siglufjordur in 1997. It is not only a work of technology but also of art, relating to the site and serving as a panoramic promenade for local residents.

Projects

Cap Roig residential development

Programme Master plan and
details for a square and park
in a new housing development
Designer Michèle & Miquel
Architectes & Paisatgistes
Client Institut Català del Sól
Area 5.4 ha
Design period 2001
Implementation period
2003-2004
Cost € 562,000

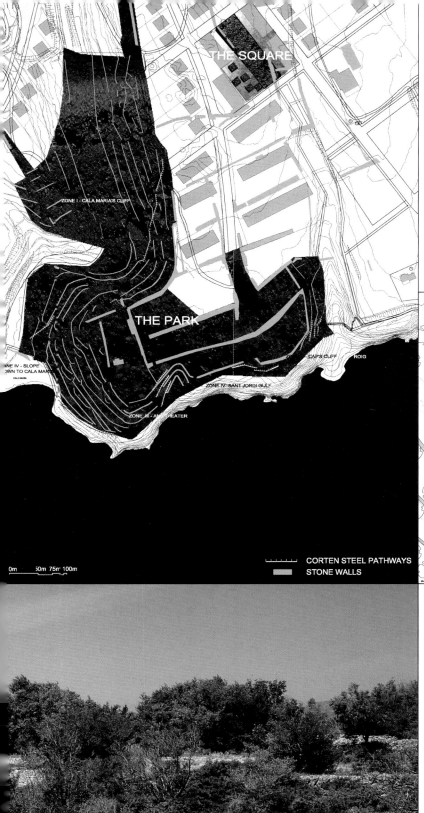

THE SQUARE

ZONE I - CALA MARIA'S CLIFF

THE PARK

NE IV - SLOPE
WN TO CALA MAR
CALA MARI

CAP'S CLIFF   ROIG

ZONE IV- SANT JORDI GULF

ZONE III - AMPITHEATER

0m   50m 75m 100m

CORTEN STEEL PATHWAYS
STONE WALLS

‹   The two parts of the site. The smaller is the village square, the larger the public park.
▾   Detail of the introduction of Corten steel paths connecting the old stone walls and forming
    an open air theatre.
‹ ▾   View of the completed situation in the park area. Subtle fusion of old and new natural
    materials. (Photo: Lourdes Jansana)

In a former olive grove on the Mediterranean coast a new housing
development has been wonderfully integrated into the surroundings
in a careful interpretation of the qualities of the local topography.
The designers were brought into the planning of the site when the plot
layout and access system had already been drawn in, but the public
open spaces were still blank. The design consists of two main elements:
a landscaped square in the centre of the neighbourhood and a park
on the cliff, enclosed by two dry gullies and the sea.

In the jury's opinion, the treatment of the site exhibits considerable
landscape architectural skill and a keen eye for the functional and
sculptural potential of the site. The design avoided levelling the site
as originally planned, leaving the relief intact. The result was a strikingly
sharp contrast between the level streets and the rolling and uneven olive
groves in between. This treatment has revealed interesting differences in
ground level, sometimes held in place by retaining walls, and allows the
old olive trees to live on as icons of the transformed landscape. The
walls are made of concrete mixed with local soil to give it the typical
red colour of the earth. The square has in fact become a garden and
the compartmentalized relief lends it a spontaneous and intimate feel.
In the evenings, lighting built into the long, modular concrete benches
bathes the square in a subdued light. This relatively simple treatment
allowed the public garden to be completed before the housing.

The design for the park at the edge of the neighbourhood was heavily
inspired by the numerous old retaining walls, which hold up the olive
terraces, some four metres thick. These groves line the coast like a

73

- › Setting of the square in the urban area. Strong contrast between levelled and untouched terrain.
- ‒ Section through the smaller width of the square. The visibility of the local topography is enhanced.
- ≋ Detail of the completed situation. Olive trees are spared and monumentalized.

series of dry paddies. The site layout leaves this old structure intact and adds a contemporary layer which makes a minimal impact. The plan includes a walk between the higher areas and the coastline. A path for swimmers, sunbathers and anglers; no more and no less. The route of the path takes in the old retaining walls but does not expose them to excessive wear and tear. In places where the path needs to be marked out, Corten steel plates of 1.5 by three metres have been folded and mounted to form steps or a bench. These plates can be found in five places along the cliffs. They stand out as parallel lines in the slope, but their rust-red colour blends easily into the background. At the half-way point in the route they form a small open air theatre.

The selection committee was unanimous in its approval of this design and the way it has been realized on the ground. The interpretation of the landscape made a valuable correction to the original plan and has delivered a neighbourhood with a strong identity. Everyone benefits.

Corten steel retaining wall forming pathways in the park area. (Photo: Lourdes Jansana)

Strong contrast between existing topography and new street level.

View from Cap Roig over the Mediterranean Sea.

75

De Nieuwe Ooster cemetery

Programme Multiple assignment for transformation of a cemetery
Designer Karres en Brands landschapsarchitecten bv
In collaboration with Rod'or Advies (technical advise)
Client De Nieuwe Ooster cemetery, crematorium and memorial park
Area 33 ha
Design period 2003-2004
Implementation period 2005 onward
Cost € 1,600,000

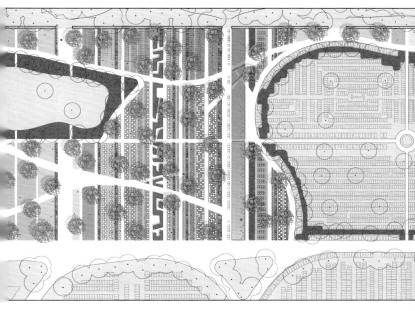

Cemeteries were and are mirrors of our society. They represent the relation between the collective and the individual and the social hierarchy. They reflect current ideas both on nature as well as on death, burial and reminiscence. They also express developments in park and landscape architecture. The design for the transformation of De Nieuwe Ooster cemetery in Amsterdam was therefore more than just an isolated stylistic exercise. It demanded a clear spatial intervention coupled to a vision on how and in which physical context people nowadays prefer to be buried or cremated or how relatives and friends want to part from a loved one.

In the original design from landscape architect Springer the ideas of that time complied fully with the layering of society. The graves of the wealthy lay along the curved pathways. At crossings accentuated with groups of trees, the special graves were situated and in the open fields were the graves of the less prosperous. In the first extension of 1915, also designed by Springer, a clear change can be seen. Here the emphasis lies more on identity and experience of singular grave fields. The planting edges enclose grave meadows, making the character of the second part more uniform. The second extension was designed by the Municipal Office for Public Works and is slightly out of place. This part of the cemetery is inspired by Springer but lacks structure and identity. It is a collection of loose fragments, showing that the demand for more diverse ways of burial has not been coupled to a new spatial concept for the whole zone.

Karres en Brands decided to emphasize the difference in atmosphere and layout of the three parts, by enhancing the contrasts. For the most recent

‹   View along one of the long lines in the design.
‹ ▲ Masterplan for a linear organization of grave fields and burial wall. Contrast with the original park layout.
⇕   Aerial view of the Nieuwe Ooster cemetry.
▲   Spatial strategy for three different zones of the cemetery. Spatial development scheme for the most recent part.

▲ Temporary flower beds.
▾ Pedestrian bridge over the pond.

extension they have proposed a new identity that expresses an emancipated, non-hierarchical, individualized society. Their structure plan offers an extremely flexible and very informal scheme, inspired by the extended Springer norm that "everyone buried can lie along a pathway". The organizational base is a zone with parallel strips of different widths, design and materialization, aligned by footpaths. In several strips there are hedges dividing the whole zone in spatial compartments. The existing grave fields and the ash fields are incorporated in the zone as large irregular chambers with green borders. In the whole zone, loosely scattered, stand birch trees. Two strips have a special significance and provide gardenesque accents. One is the undulated, incised and perforated burial wall. It presents itself as a huge piece of curved furniture with interior and exterior compartments for ash urns. The other special strip is the pond which gives space to the site and provides a unique place to commit ashes.

The selection committee was charmed by the combination of the brutal scheme and the skilful detailing of the plan. The escape from traditional cemetery design is convincing, both tempting and controversial. The qualities and potential of the new layout are beautifully illustrated.

▸ ▴ Basalt pedestals for urn pots and vases.
▸ ▴ Elevation model of the columbarium. Intimacy without closure.
▸ Test of the columbarium.
▸▸ Impression of the inside of the burial wall.

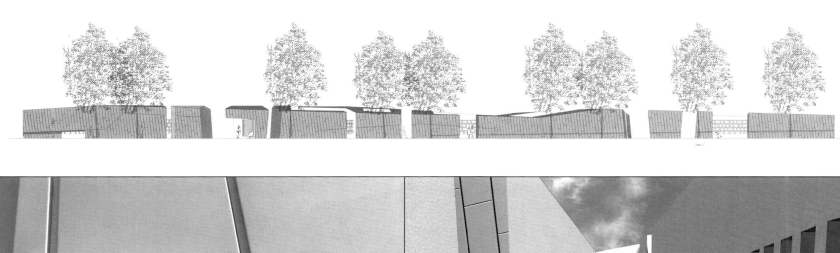

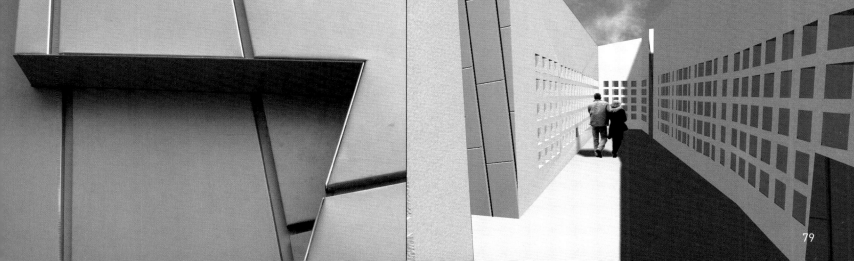

Monnikenhuizen settlement

Programme Landscape plan,
detailing and materialisation
for a new residential area of
204 dwellings
Designer BURO LUBBERS
landschapsarchitectuur en
stedelijk ontwerp
In collaboration with
Khandekar b.v. (urban concept),
Atelier Z,
Meyer & Van Schoten,
Van de Looi & Jacobs, Vera
Yanovshtchinsky (architecture)
Client Johan Matser
Projectontwikkeling bv
and municipality of Arnhem
Area 6.5 ha
Design period 1998-1999
Implementation period
2000-2001
Cost € 3,700,000

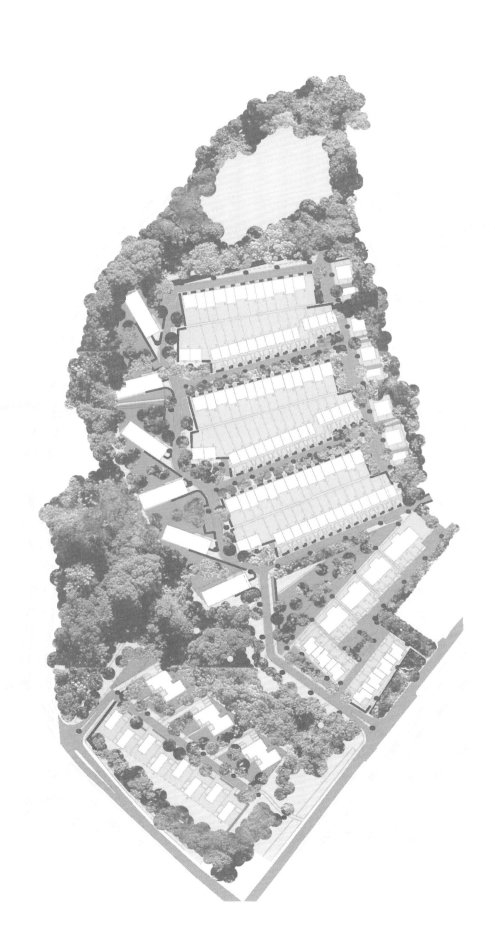

› Overall plan. Two different
residential "rooms" separated
by a green corridor.
›▲ View of the triangular pond in
the centre of the neighbourhood.
Gabions create a specific
atmosphere.
›› Component parts of the
landscape design. Infiltration
network, gabions between private
and public, birch trees, green
fields, oak trees, rhododendrons,
gabions to overcome height
differences, stairs and bridges,
gutters and pond.

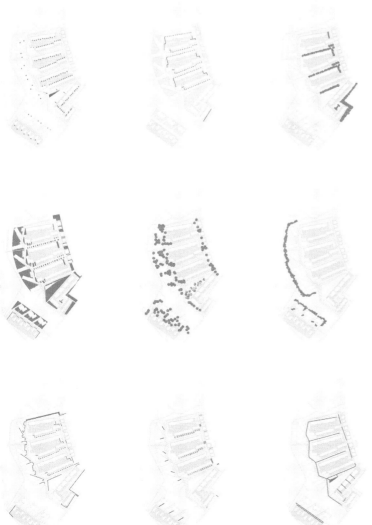

The area of Monnikenhuizen is located on the former grounds of the Arnhem soccer club Vitesse and between the two old country estates Angerenstein and Klarenbeek. The undulating terrain and wooded landscape provided an unprecedented asset for the development of an attractive neighbourhood in close relation with its surroundings. A total of 204 dwellings were built with a mixture of apartments, terraced houses and villas. The urban master plan introduced two 'rooms' in the forest: a large room with lines of houses on four terraces and with cul-de-sacs, and a smaller room containing detached and semi-detached houses. The dead end streets are wide enough to serve as parking area and to function as loop to make a turn. Stairs connect the cul-de-sacs with each other and footpaths lead to a more elevated pathway through the forest. Between the two rooms the landscape was redeveloped to serve as an ecological corridor between the two country estates.

Three landscape elements are crucial for the identity and atmosphere of this project: the introduction of gabions, the visibility of the water system and the generous tree planting. The natural topography – with differences in elevation up to 24 meters at the edges of the two rooms – asked for the application of retaining walls to hold back the loose sand. Blocks of dry rock in gabion form were used to create a semi-natural feature that had a strongly unifying impact on the whole project. In dialogue with the architects the gabions were integrated in the foundations of the houses, implemented in façades and used as garden separations. The whole system of water collection, storage, transportation and infiltration has been made explicit and visible. The water structure serves as speed ramps in streets, offers playing possibilities and scenic qualities. Broad

▸ A gabion landscape for living.
▾ Gabions integrated in the architecture.
▸▾ The pond as a focal point in the neighbourhood.

grooves in the walls of the houses channel the rainwater down where a system of large gutters in the middle of the pavement carry the water to the triangular infiltration pond located in the middle of the neighbourhood. Trees were generously planted. The streets have asymmetrical profiles. A wide verge planted with hundreds of birch trees results in a highly green and natural streetscape. The streets are wide enough to integrate everyday elements such as cars, bicycles and waste containers. Around the urban villas patches of *Rhododendron* and a clump of oak were planted as a reference to the two estates.

The jury selected this project because of the richness in layering and the homely atmosphere of the site. Monnikenhuizen has won several prizes in the Netherlands. Its development shows that spatial coherence in contemporary urban development not always depends on the introduction of a grand and formal design of a road and parcelling scheme but can also be achieved through a strict selection and skilful materialization of outdoor physical components.

- Gabions as retaining walls with stairs leading to the woods.
- Residents cross bridges to reach the apartments on the south side. Cars are parked in the basement.
- Birch trees mark and camouflage the parking spaces.

Location Athens (GR)

Hellenikon Metropolitan Park

Programme Urban and
landscape master plan of
Athens international airport
Designer David Serero and
Elena Fernandez, Iterae
Architecture, and Philippe
Coignet, Office of Landscape
Morphology
In collaboration with
Erwin Redl (artist)
Client Greek Ministry of
Environment, Planning and
Public Works

Area 530 ha
Design period 2004
Implementation period
2005-2020
Cost € 700,000,000

0 50 100 150 200

Hellenikon is the old Athens civil airport, which closed in 2001. Located on The Seronic Gulf some 20 kilometres west of Athens, the site was a venue for the 2004 Olympic Games. From 2003 to 2004 the Greek Minister for the Environment sponsored an open international competition for a "21st century urban park of exceptional scale and remarkable design". The programme included housing, offices and social services on 125 hectares and a park with "green areas, cultural, sports and leisure facilities". The brief required the new urban development to generate enough income to finance the park and required the restoration of the Eero Saarinen main terminal, built in 1960.

In May 2004, the Iterae/OLM project won first prize in the design competition for an urban park, which would be larger than Central Park, New York. In 2005 the Ministry of the Environment asked the prize winning team to develop their proposal to schematic design. The Iterae/OLM design strategy is based on rainwater collection and ground modelling. They established a series of six corridors, 200 to 300 metres wide, linking the existing city, on higher ground, to the coastline 60 metres below. These corridors or "softscapes" incorporate a new drainage system as well as a network of roads, bicycle paths and walkways. This modified topography and structural landscape of corridors is both a way to improve the soil and a structure to organize the new urban areas. Housing is proposed between each corridor, providing a catalyst around which further residential, commercial and leisure development will occur.

- Proposed view of runway crossing a softscape.
- Six softscape corridors link the existing city on higher ground to the coastline 60 metres below.
- The main runway alignments are retained as structural elements in the new masterplan.

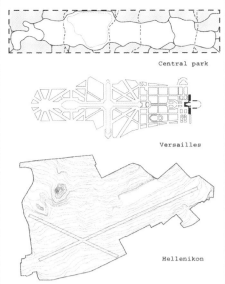

Central park

Versailles

Hellenikon

The softscape corridors use planting and storm water management to catch, store and release rainwater through a system of terraces, embankments and retaining walls that create level areas for various activities. The main airport runway is retained, defining a visual and circulation axis that links the six softscapes. The second and smaller runway will be extended towards the sea as a huge belvedere and pier.

The tree planting strategy is related to wet and dry ground conditions and involves creation of a range of new habitats and ecological types. Initially garrigue type vegetation will be established with a few species being used to colonize the internal part of the softscapes. This pioneer garrigue vegetation of Mediterranean shrubs will prepare the ground for future mature woodland (pine, olive and oak) adapted to a Mediterranean climax community. Of course vegetation will vary, according to habitat and maintenance level. The aim is not to structure every aspect of the 550 hectares, but more to organize a set of conditions and habitats (ground, slopes and water surfaces) to create the park and develop an integrated system that can accommodate developments over a twenty-year period. The jury saw this as a "very powerful" project which involves "weaving things together... it's about scale".

▸ ▴ Plans of Central Park New York, Versailles and Hellenikon on the same scale.
▴ The design is structured around six softscape corridors leading to the coast and the former runways.
▸ (from top to bottom)
Areas for activities (elements of "programmatic noise", hardscapes, edges maximize frontages, softscapes.

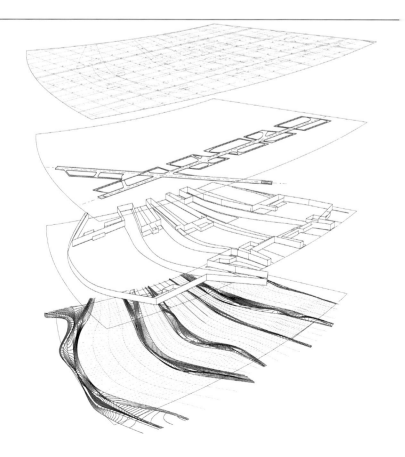

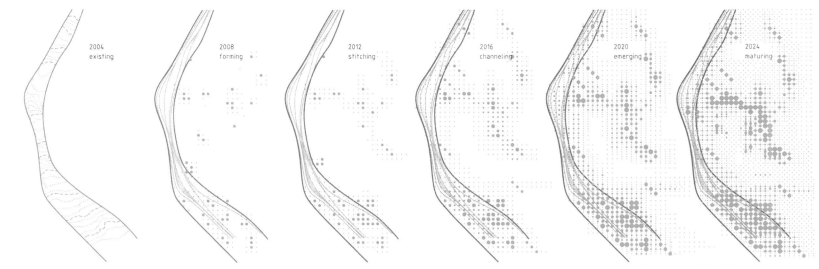

2004 existing	2008 forming	2012 stitching	2016 channeling	2020 emerging	2024 maturing

⮝ The natural succession will take over 20 years following an ecological succession.

⬝ The Seronic Gulf on the left and the old airfield site are a major development site for the Athens conurbation.

◂ Garrigue-type Mediterranean shrub vegetation developing to pine and oak woodland climax vegetation.

Location Bad Essen (D)

Garden of Babel

Programme Temporary garden
installation in the park at
Schloss Ippenburg
Designer
Klahn + Singer + Partner
Client Viktoria Freifrau von
dem Bussche
Area 1,500 m²
Design period 1999
Implementation period
2000-2001
Cost € 10,000

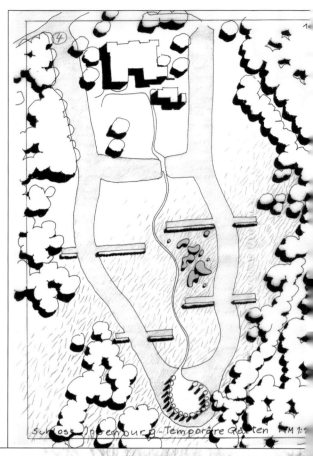

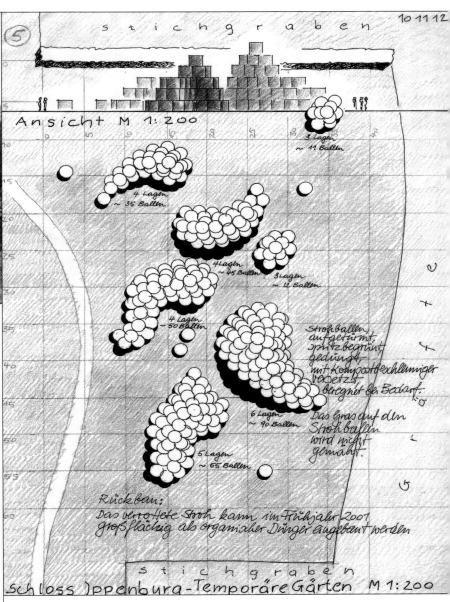

Privately organized garden festivals of importance have been taking place at Ippenburg Castle in the Westphalian town of Bad Essen since 1998. The owner of the Neo-Gothic castle and its extensive English-style park wants to enliven her historic monument. She therefore invites landscape designers and artists every year to create temporary landscapes. A jury of landscape architecture pros selects the gardens to be realized. They are open to the public from spring to autumn, and they have brought Ippenburg Castle the reputation of being a centre for landscape design.

All gardens are temporary gardens, the landscape architects of Klahn + Singer + Partner believe. They created a garden at Ippenburg Castle between 2000 and 2001 that you could call "a built manifesto of the profession" straight out. At least that is how the jury of the present publication formulated it. In this work, the jurors saw composition and growth, change and decay, revival and the entire dramatic art of the designed landscape. They allowed themselves to be captivated by the beauty and power of this garden, whose materials are so modest, so ephemeral and yet so eloquent that they make the brevity of the garden's existence clear to you: "Wonderful, how this work stands there, speaks to you, how it then decays, and all that in a single season – very romantic and strong."

The landscape architects called their project Garden of Babel with reference to the painting by Pieter Bruegel the Elder that shows the construction of a massive tower, ambitiously striving heavenward – and the failure of the undertaking. An allegory for the limits of human designs. These limits are what the landscape architects experience every single

«▲ Situation of the Garden of Babel within the gardens of Schloss Ippenburg.
‹▲ View from the straw bales towards the Neo-Gothic Castle.
▲ Ground plan and frontal sketch.
(Photos: Ulrich Singer)

day in dealing with natural materials and natural processes, and incorporate into their work as a matter of course – an attitude that certainly differentiates them from architects, not only those of The Tower of Babel. The landscape architects even take pleasure in playing with the limits of their activity with no frustration whatsoever. In a clearing in Ippenburg Castle Park, Klahn + Singer + Partner piled up straw bales into shapes that recall the broad tower in Brueghel's painting. At least 11 bales in three storeys, at most 90 bales in six storeys result in a composition that fills the space and can be wandered through and admired. Sprayed with grass seed and fertilized, the masses are quickly covered with furry green grass in spring, which is watered as needed over the summer, but on no account mowed. The landscape architects included decay in the project from the start. Grass and compost accelerator induce the process of decomposition, the changes toward autumn, through the winter and into the next spring, so that nothing remains of the composition but piles of decayed straw that can be used as organic fertilizer in the castle park.

At first, the piled-up straw bales look no different from what you find everywhere in the area: agricultural produce stacked up in the fields. As soon as they are covered with grass, however, the hard-edged relief disappears and the shapes acquire a live aspect, like a big animal, a furry fabulous creature, almost surreal. The landscape architects were thinking of Meret Oppenheim's fur cup, known by the name of *"Le Déjeuner en fourrure"*, dating from 1936. By covering them with fur, Oppenheim bestowed something live on a cup, a saucer and a spoon, her faithful breakfast companions at the Parisian Café de Flore. Similarly, the landscape architects animate the material they work with and make it into – if not an antagonist – then in any case a supporting actor.

> Pieter Brueghel the Elder's painting "The Tower of Babel" has been used as a reference by the landscape architects.

▲ Construction: freshly piled up straw bales.

◄ Growth: over the summer, the straw bales get covered with grass.

▼ Decomposition: decaying straw bales in autumn.

Plaza del Desierto

Programme Design for public
open space between apartment
buildings
Designer
NOMAD Arquitectos S.L.
Client Bilbao Ría 2000
Area 1.2 ha
Design period 1998–1999
Implementation period
2000–2002
Cost € 1,500,000

■	100% water
□	100% stone
▨	100% asphalt
□	100% sand
▨	100% green
▨	100% forrest
▨	100% steel
▨	100% wood
▨	50% green 50% forrest
▨	50% green 50% wood
▨	50% green 50% steel
▨	50% stone 50% forrest
▨	50% stone 50% green
▨	50% sand 50% steel
▨	50% sand 50% wood
▨	50% steel 50% wood
▨	50% water 50% green
□	50% water 50% stone
▨	50% water 50% wood
▨	50% stone 50% sand
▨	50% stone 50% wood
▨	50% sand 50% forrest
▨	50% asphalt 50% green
■	50% water 50% asphalt
▨	50% stone 50% asphalt
▨	50% asphalt 50% forrest
▨	33% water 33% stone 33% green
□	33% stone 33% green 33% forrest

Eduardo Arroyo of NOMAD Arquitectos in Madrid caused quite a stir with his design for the Plaza del Desierto in Barakaldo, a medium-sized town in the Basque country. Just a glance at the drawings is enough to see that Arroyo has not turned out any ordinary design. His design won the open competition organized by Bilbao Ría 2000 in 1999. Bilbao Ría 2000 is a public body responsible for major projects in the region, such as the Guggenheim Museum.

The designer's core idea for the vacant lot in the middle of the yet to be built apartment complex was recalling history. Given the current level of interest in cultural history and demand for plans that draw inspiration from the past, this is not entirely original. But Eduardo Arroyo quite literally puts memories of far-off days back into the square. In the past the site has been home to a farming settlement, shipyards and then steel factories. Materials from these different activities have been found in and around the site. These materials, including wood, chalk, steel, asphalt and clay as well as tree remains, water and "green" elements, have been arranged in a spatial composition. The designer laid a regular rectangular topographic grid, complete with differences in elevation, over the site. Each rectangle was allocated a material or combination of materials, depending on where they were found and on practical requirements such as amount of sunlight, lighting, viewpoints, or simply the need for access for emergency services. The result is a mysterious mixture of recovered remains scattered over the site. To describe his method Arroyo uses the word superposición: overlapping. By this he means that the materials, however different in nature and age, are not separated from each other, but integrated.

◄ View of Plaza del Desierto.
▲ A colourful grid forms the basis of the design.
▼ One of the many places to sit in the square.
(Photos: Roland Halbe)

Translating such an abstract plan into an easily negotiable and functional square places heavy demands on the construction work. Arroyo brought in architects, engineers and a landscape architect to help transform the materials into elements of the square and the park. They have created a wide variety of benches, decking, hard surfacing, fountains, bushes, tree clusters, bridges, water features, steps, lanterns and planting holes.

This idiosyncratic working method has resulted in a public domain that seems to hang together by chance, and yet displays a certain coherence. Desert Plaza is an exciting labyrinth that imposes no single type of use. Shady benches offer space for romance, the elderly linger for a chat, and perhaps there are children playing in the shallow ponds, while skaters take full advantage of the slopes. These are expectations; even the designer is not sure how his brainchild will be used.

The selection committee was immediately taken by the somewhat arcane drawings. A wonderful composition. The committee praises the intelligent use of a layered topography and mix of vegetation and hard materials.

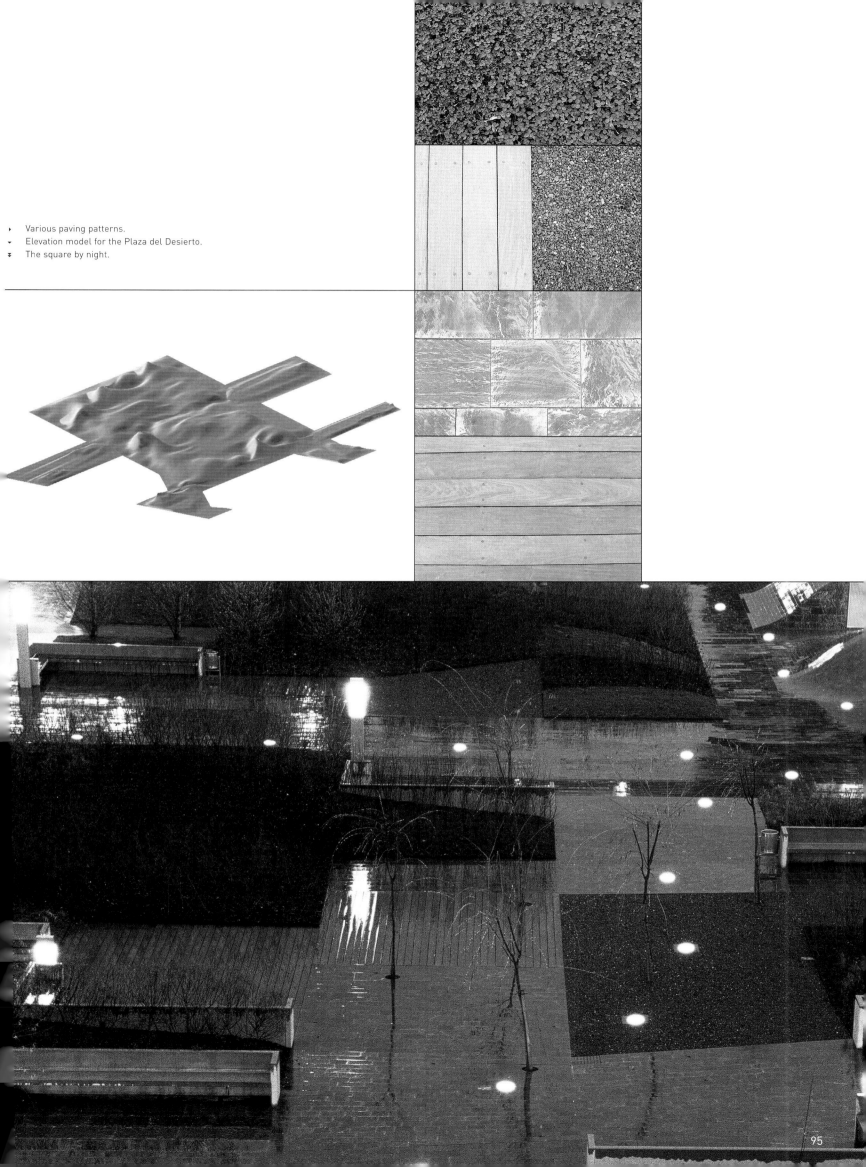

▸ Various paving patterns.
▾ Elevation model for the Plaza del Desierto.
⇕ The square by night.

95

Location Berlin (D)

Open spaces in the Spreebogen government district

Programme Design for the
open spaces in the Spreebogen
government district
Designer Cornelia Müller and
Jan Wehberg, Lützow 7 Garten-
und Landschaftsarchitekten
Client Federal State of Berlin,
Federal Republic of Germany
Area 28 ha
Design period 1996
Implementation period
1998-2004
Cost € 12,000,000

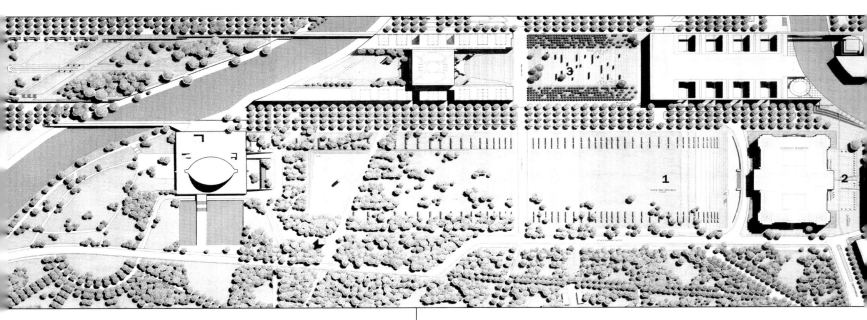

When Berlin grew back together again after the Wall came down, the so-called Band des Bundes (federal government strip) stood for the union of East and West. The area to the north of the Tiergarten, in a curve of the River Spree, was to be the site of the new government district according to the master plan by the architects Axel Schultes and Charlotte Frank. They lined up the Chancellor's office, ministries and federal institutions in a row that ran straight from east to west, crossing the river twice and linking architecturally what was once divided. The master plan for the federal government strip was subsequently further elaborated and supplied with representative buildings by various architects. However, not only buildings were to shape the basic urban design. In 1996 the public authorities held a design competition for the new government district's open spaces. The point was to find a form on the one hand for the Bürgerforum (Citizens' Forum), an open space spreading from the Chancellor's office to the House of the Members of Parliament of the GDR, and on the other for the Platz der Republik, which borders the federal government strip to the south and extends from the *Haus der Kulturen der Welt* (House of World Cultures) in the Tiergarten to the front of the former Reichstag (rebuilt by Sir Norman Foster into the Parliament building). In addition, a design was required for Friedrich-Ebert-Platz, which to some extent creates a transition from behind the Parliament building to the city district of Berlin-Mitte.

The first prize went to Cornelia Müller and Jan Wehberg of the Berlin office, Lützow 7. Their design not only does justice to the site's significance as the stronghold of democracy but also to its location at the transition between the free forms of the Tiergarten designed by Peter

▲ The German government institutions are situated on Band des Bundes crossing the river Spree twice. Between the Chancellor's office and the House of the Members of Parliament, the landscape architects created the Bürgerforum (3). To the south they shaped Republic Square (1) as a green strip in front of the former Reichstag, the present Parliament building. Behind this Friedrich Ebert Square (2) connects with the Mitte city district.

◄ Aerial view of Band des Bundes. (Foto: Artur)

▼ Hawthorn hedges lead to the corners of the Reichstag building.

- ▲ For the representation of democracy the lightness of the tree groves is juxtaposed with the rigidity of the formal hedgerows and concrete steps framing the central lawn of Republic Square.
- ▸▲ View towards the Reichtag building.
- ▾ View towards the Band des Bundes.

Joseph Lenné in the English landscape style and the linear urban design gesture of the federal government strip. In order to lend appropriate expression to the idea of democracy, the landscape architects wanted to create open spaces suitable for various uses. All three open spaces give the impression of spaciousness and openness: Platz der Republik through its level central lawn, the Bürgerforum through its simple parallel structure of strips of paving and lawn, and Friedrich-Ebert-Platz through its regular paving with large-sized stone tiles.

With informally placed tree clusters of maple, ash and linden, Platz der Republik continues the character of the Tiergarten at its southern edge. Towards the Parliament building, solitaires escape from the tree clusters, and on the side of the *Haus der Kulturen der Welt*, they blend completely naturally into the straight rows of trees along Paul-Löbe-Allee at the northern edge. The landscape architects enclose the three-hectare lawn on both the north and south sides with hawthorn hedges (*Crataegus prunifolia*) in a parallel alignment, leading in the form of a 16-metre-wide strip to the corner towers of the Reichstag building and emphasizing its architectonic order with a mathematically determined rhythm. The planners bundle the hedges in the direction of the building, placing the rows increasingly closely together until they form a dense architectural mass.

At the back of the Parliament building, Friedrich-Ebert-Platz forms a stone counterpart to the green carpet of the Platz der Republik. With two-by-two-metre monolithic slabs, the landscape architects continue the monumental order of the building in the open space. Despite their weight,

▲ The hedges interfere with solitaire trees that seem to escape from the wooden masses of Tiergarten.
◄ Design drawing of Republic Square in front of, and Friedrich Ebert Square behind the Reichstag.
▼ At the northern edge of Friedrich Ebert Square, flight of steps lead to the banks of river Spree.

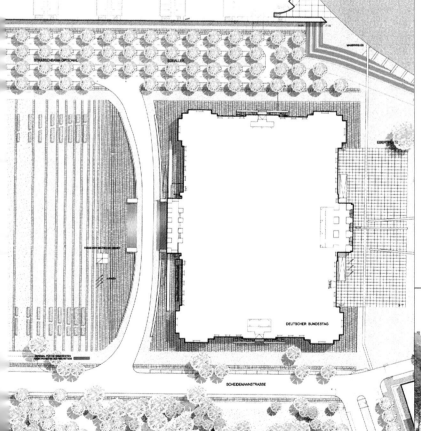

▸ | » Two-by-two metre monolithic slabs repeat the monumental order of the Reichstag
building and seem to float above the surface of the square, especially when lit at night.
▴   Linear fountains add curtains and the sound of water. [Photo: Andreas Muhs]
▸ ⌄ Design drawing.

some of the slabs seem to float above the surface of the square, set off by a joint that shines at night thanks to integrated lighting. The slabs invite people to take a seat. Poured-in-place concrete segments trace the course of the Berlin Wall.

The planners designed the Bürgerforum as a place for encounters. Parallel strips of lawn and pavement form a rhythmic pattern that acquires a third dimension through linear fountains rising from the stone surfaces. Solitaire sugar maples (*Acer saccharum*) are scattered throughout the severely designed area in an informal composition. To close off the southern and northern limits, the landscape architects planted maple clusters that can shelter stalls and seating.

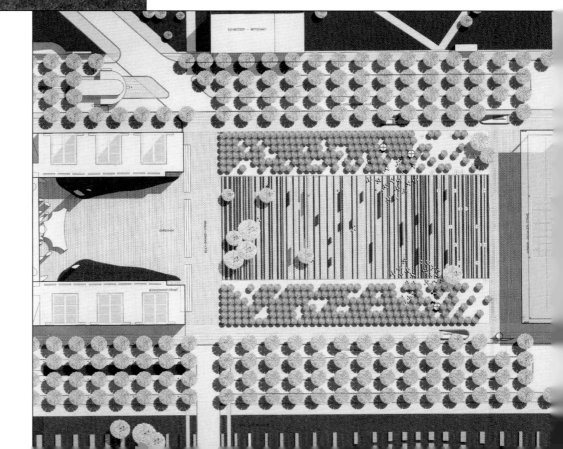

Friedrich Ebert Square.
The Bürgerforum is composed of a rhythm of parallel strips of lawn and pavement.

Tilla Durieux public park

Programme A long grass sculpture rotated on its axis
Designer DS Landschapsarchitecten
In collaboration with Thomas M. Dietrich, Berlin
Client City Council Mitte Berlin
Area 2.5 ha
Design period 1995-2003
Implementation period 2002–2003
Cost € 2,500,000

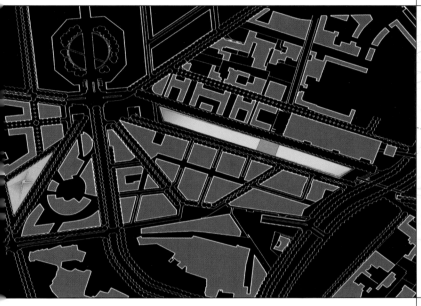

- Plan.
- Technical drawing.
- The 450-metre long park from the air. (Photo: Hans Joosten)

The fall of the Berlin Wall in 1989 not only opened the doors between East and West Berlin, it also opened up opportunities for the development and use of the strip of land where the Wall once stood. One of the best known sites is the area around the Potsdamer Platz, which has developed into a vibrant new economic and tourist centre. In no time, this young district has acquired a cosmopolitan character. This was reflected in the architecture, which in some ways may even be called megalomaniacal. The architecture gives the area vigour, but also threatened to dominate the public space. It was necessary, during the planning and construction of the buildings, to make plans for high quality open space. Potential sites were already available, such as the Prachtgleis, a rectangular area between the office buildings, and the Kemper Park.

In 1995 the Berlin city administration held an international design competition for these two sites. The district surrounding Potsdamer Platz was to be given two new parks to compensate for the overbearing buildings and provide a quiet place to unwind.

DS Landschapsarchitecten in Amsterdam were convincing winners of the competition. Henriette Herz Park (formerly Kemper Park) was opened in 2002. In 2003 Tilla Durieux Park in the Prachtgleis area was completed and opened. This park stretches for more than 450 metres, flanked by promenades and the facades of the apartment buildings. It runs from Potsdamer Platz at one end to the Landwehrkanal water course at the other. DS submitted only its design for the Tilla Durieux Park to consider for inclusion in this book.

The park is a 30-metre wide grass sculpture. It is best described as a sloping embankment that rotates around its longitudinal axis. At a certain point on one side the grass slope seems to disappear beneath the street, while just a few hundred metres further on it towers four metres above street level. At the first point the slope is easily negotiated, but at the second point you face a metres-high bank. In the middle the mound is interrupted by a small square. This is surrounded by steel retaining walls. The square, paved with black basalt cobbles, links the two promenades and provides a play area for young and old. Five stainless steel see-saws have been mounted above moulded rubber mats, so that anyone who wishes can rise and dip with the grassy bank. The promenades on either side of the sculpture have been planted with European linden (*Tilia x europaea Pallida)* and horse chestnut trees. A walk along these rows of trees brings the impression of a rotating movement to life.

What makes the Tilla Durieux Park really special is that it is not designed and laid out in the way you expect for a park. There are no fences around it and it does not have any one obvious entrance point or any pathways. But it is still considered to be a park and people use it as such. In sunny weather the park is strewn with people either sunbathing or reading books. Such functional aspects of the park are less evident in the autumn and winter. During these seasons, say the designers, it can become a snow-white sculpture or a misty meadow.

The selection committee agreed that this is an intelligent concept that perfectly complements the city centre environment of Potsdamer Platz. Although some committee members can imagine the office workers on the first floors become tired of looking out at a green wall, the jury was enthusiast about the impact of the park. It has a sturdy form that can hold its own against the gigantic buildings. It creates space; people can breathe again.

- The central part with the five stainless steel seesaws. (Photo: Jens Schulz)
- The slopes of the park are a wonderful play area for children.
- The park is flanked by European lindens. (Photo: Aeliane van den Ende)

◢ Students and office workers
   relax on the green slopes.
▸ The promenade.
   (Photos: Jens Schulz)

Jardin Botanique

Programme Design of the
Botanical Garden in the new
urban development district
La Bastide
Designer Mosbach Paysagistes
In collaboration with Jourda
Architectes (architecture),
P. Blanc, P. Richard (botany),
Phytoconseil (horticulture),
R. Seroni (geology)
Client City of Bordeaux
Area 4.6 ha
Design period 2000

Implementation period
2001-2005
Cost € 7,200,000

esplanade des quinconces

g a r o n n e   r i v e r

grand
théâtre

place
de la
bourse

place
du
parlement

new neighbourhood

place
de
Stalingrad

A botanical garden translates a didactic programme: to exhibit natural landscapes, cultural landscapes and experiments in greenhouses. Yet, that is not all, at least not in Bordeaux. The landscape architect Catherine Mosbach won the competition for the New Botanical Garden of Bordeaux in 1999 with a design for the characteristics of which she drew mainly on her own world of ideas. To her mind, making people acquainted with the relationship between nature and culture in the centre of town could only succeed in a landscape space that is intellectually understood and emotionally moving at the same time. A space that welcomes visitors not only to research but also to saunter, and where those out for a stroll are drawn into the world of botany even without signs and information panels. Fulfilling the didactic programme was compulsory for the landscape architect. Revealing the poetry and the content of these spaces to the public challenged her to a risky optional exercise. According to the jury, she achieved the essential goals: making the water into a mirror, the rocks into diamonds, the fields into gardens, and combining these three completely different elements into a single, sensitive garden of longing.

To begin with, Mosbach understood the opening of the garden in terms of urban space. Dominique Perrault's master plan for the La Bastide development area assigned the Botanical Garden an elongated narrow lot, 70 metres wide, extending from the bank of the Garonne to the old Sainte-Marie church. New office and residential buildings adjoin it on either side. A self-contained medieval botanical collection could not have been squeezed in here. Mosbach therefore developed the garden as a showcase with fluid borders to the city and the river. She enclosed the garden with a ha-ha, a depression bordered by a low embankment. The

‹ View from the Botanical Garden towards the historical waterfront across the River Garonne.
⚈ The ground plan takes over the historical grid of the agricultural land of the La Bastide district.
▲ View from the "Water Garden" towards Sainte-Marie church.

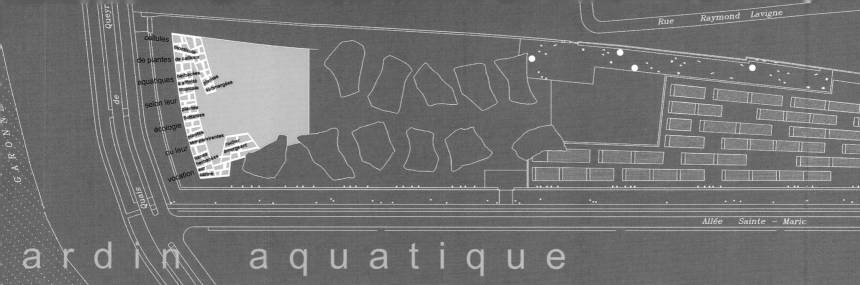

- Ground plan of the "Water Garden".
- Metal plates border the pool of the "Water Garden".
- Aerial view of the "Water Garden" and the "Gallery of Natural Landscapes".

one-metre wide embankment consists of oak planks, relics of the storm of 1999, stacked on top of each other and colonized by pioneer growth: mosses, lichen, ferns, as well as gold moss or stonecrop (*Sedum acre*). People can see this "Pioneer Trail" (*sentier des pionnières*) from both outside and in, and can look over the top of it from the garden into the city and vice versa – a boundary that has turned into a landscape. Down towards the bank of the Garonne, the "Water Garden" (jardin aquatique) forms another edge. A net of metal plates surrounds a large pool and many smaller ones, altogether one hectare in area. Plants flourish between water and air on protruding rocks, cabbage-like climbing plants (*Ipomaea sagittata, subrevoluta* and *squamosa*) rise up and attract the ducks, large tropical-looking plants (*Pontederia lanceolata, Saururus chinensis, Alisma parviflorum*) grow in underwater planters, and water lilies spread out their leaves and flowers only in the summer. Finally, at the opposite end of the Botanical Garden, the "Urban Garden" (jardin urbain) leads over into the neighbourhood. Here the garden becomes architecture: the architect Francoise-Hélène Jourda used organically shaped building modules to build the greenhouses and the administration and museum centre.

Inner openness was just as important to Mosbach as permeability toward the city. She therefore did not prescribe a precise tour. She organized the garden into three zones: the "Urban Garden", the "Field of Crops" (*champ de cultures*) and the "Gallery of Natural Landscapes" (*galerie des milieux*). She arranged the corresponding garden elements informally on the ground of the elongated lot. Anyone can go through them freely. The "Field of Crops" shows the cultivated plants of world agricultures on

The informally arranged cut-outs of different environments of the Aquitaine basin in front of the "Water Garden".

Ground plan of the "Gallery of Natural Landscapes".

extraits de paysages du bassin Aquitain dans leur formation géologique, pédologique et végétale
paysages acides en rive gauche de la Garonne

paysages calcaires en rive droite de la Garonne

Rue Raymond Lavigne

Allée Sainte - Marie

↑ | › The cross sections of the elements of the "Gallery of Natural Landscapes" reveal the geological stratifications.
↓ The environments welcome visitors not only to scientific research but also to enjoy the sculptural forms of vegetation and rocks.

◄ Views of the "Field of Crops".
▼ Functional processes like irrigating and the changing aspects of the crop fields are
   considered in the design.
⩣ Ground plan of the "Field of Crops".

44 plots embedded in a lawn carpet, complemented by a pool for
irrigation, and flanked by a "sitting room" with benches in the shade
under a tree. In the first year, wheat, oats, millet and flax grew here.
The "Gallery of Natural Landscapes" presents various environments of
the Aquitaine basin. The individual landscapes look cut out and deposited
on the gravel. The cross sections reveal the geological stratification as
well as the plant communities that developed on them. The five gardens
in the north represent landscapes on the right bank of the Garonne:
the wet meadowland of the Quaternary age, the pubescent oak forest
(*Quercus pubescens*) between the ocean and the Garonne of the Tertiary,
the dry meadow of the Middle Tertiary, the open green fields and
limestone hills of the Secondary. The six gardens in the south represent
landscapes on the left bank of the Garonne, inland from the ocean: the
dunes, dune fixation forest, dune hinterland forest, ditches and pools,
dry moors and wet moors. Linking them all together, the "Avenue of
Plants" (*allée des plantes*) borders the "Gallery of Natural Landscapes".
Here creepers grow over the northern boundary of the Botanical Garden
and combine in different ways with their supports: thus, for instance,
Hydrangeaceae and *Araliaceae* show their adventitious roots,
Convolvulaceae and *Aristolochiaceae* their winding stems and
Bignoniaceae and *Liliaceae* their leaf tendrils.

extraits de cultures du monde par leur
vocation ethnobotanique:
de l'usage du végétal
et de sa fonction sociale.
parcelles irriguées par
infiltration depuis des réservoirs d'eau

Allée   Sainte - Marie

ultures

Grounds for Obermarch school

Programme Environment and
sports field for district school
Designer Stefan Koepfli,
Landscape Architect BSLA
In collaboration with Graber
& Steiger Architects ETH SIA
Client March District School
Authority
Area 2.5 ha
Design period 2000-2001
Implementation period 2001
Cost € 1,200,000

This design is for a secondary school, for 12- to 16-year olds. It is located on the edge of the River Linth flood plain in an area of former marshland marked by straight drainage ditches, lines of trees, wooden footbridges and walkways. The reclamation of the Linth marshes was a major agricultural improvement in Switzerland when the Linth was channeled in 1807. Stefan Koepfli has used these elements in the design for the surroundings to the school to create a new "middle landscape" which looks out to the land around as much as it relates to the buildings. The straight lines give a rigorous linear organisation of paths and spaces, which also reflect the modernist building forms.

The car park is set on a raised level and the gravel of the parking areas has been seeded, while the roads follow the orthogonal structure of the plan. Rows of willow trees (Salix alba) provide some shade. The schoolyard is marked by wooden walkways interrupted by platforms, which act as benches or stages. Alongside the main building a pool is set within the lines of the walkway, planted with Typha angustifolia, to recall the marshland.

At first this appears to be an extremely restrained and rigorous approach, controlled and purely functional. Yet, in fact, it is a celebration of the landscape of the area that uses an elegant set of visual clues. There is much more meaning here than first meets the eye. This could be said to be modernism pushed into contextual meaning and minimalism enhanced by the celebration of place.

◄▲ The school courtyard. This design is orthogonal, aligned on the minimalist architecture.
◄   The school courtyard viewed from the grass-seeded gravel carpark, note the green roof.
⬍   Wooden planks stacked for seasoning in the nearby fields were an inspiration in the design.
⬍   The plain of the River Linth, a flat and straight, early nineteenth century land reclamation, with rows of trees that were the inspiration for the landscape design.
▲   The wooden boardwalks of marshland in the plain of the River Linth also influenced the design.

‣ The design.
▲ The school courtyard viewed from carpark.
▾ Water basin planted with Typha angustifolia.
   (Photos: H. Helferstein)

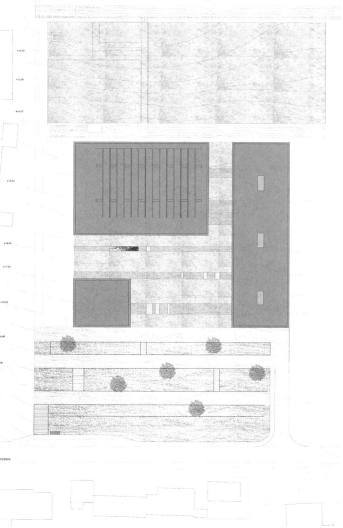

- View to the schoolyard with the timber platforms.
- Children love to rise in the world.
- The car park aligned with the building is simply arranged with gravel parking bays and unplanted roadways and simple flush edging.

Garden of the Cerca de São Bernardo

Programme Garden design
for a part of the ancient São
Bernardo enclosure
Designers Margem,
Arquitectura Paisagista Lda
In collaboration with Teixeira
Duarte Lda (construction)
Client municipality of Coimbra,
Portuguese Ministry of Culture
Area 2,750 m^2
Design period 1999-2000
Implementation period
2001-2003
Cost € 300,000

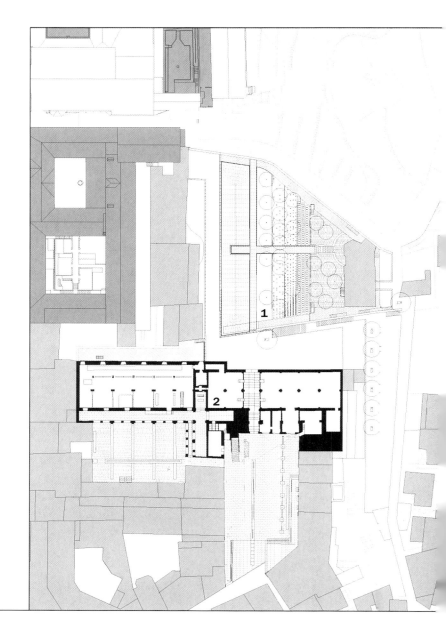

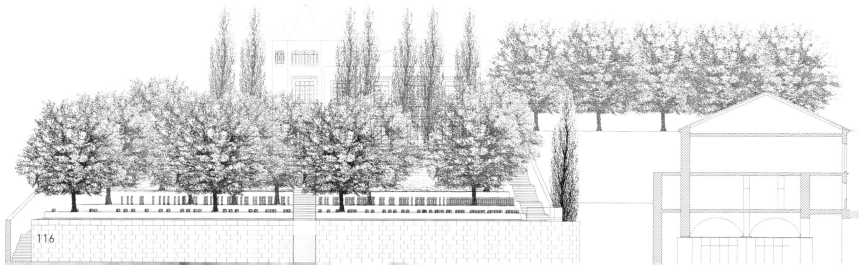

São Bernardo was built as a new university building after the University of Coimbra returned to the city in 1537. The building became the seat of the Court of the Inquisition in Coimbra and this continued until the suppression of the Inquisition in 1821. In 1999 the decision was made to house the Centre for Visual Arts here.

The gardens were originally used as a vegetable garden and for citrus orchards and are arranged in terraces which have been conserved, with the terrace walls refaced in local light buff and white limestone. The top terrace has been completely repaved in limestone and planted with columnar oak trees (*Quercus robur fastigiata*), the four terraces below have been planted with bitter orange trees (*Citrus aurantium*) and with lavender (*Lavandula dentata*), and the blue fescue grass (*Festuca ovina glauca*). At the bottom is a great pool, which crosses the whole garden. There are three routes through the garden, a stepped central axis and two perimeter sequences of steps under the high masonry walls which enclose the whole garden. The central axis descends by steps down through the four terraces and then is ramped under the water basin and will lead out to a proposed tea house. The eastern steps lead down to a metal pier over the basin while the western steps lead out of the gardens.

The jury was attracted by the scheme's subtlety and the way that "when you descend your eye is at water level" and found the detail beautiful. The scheme is strong in its main design and becomes more and more interesting. In short it is "apparently traditional, but with something new added".

Ground plan for the garden of the Cerca (1) and the Center for Visual Arts (2).
Elevation with it fastigiated oak on the top terrace and citrus on the lower terraces.
Rubble stone terraces rise to the College building.
The pool at the bottom which forms the focus of the terraced garden.

- ▲ The central axis of steps sets up a symmetry, which leads down to the future tea house and crosses this "green box" in the city.
- ↟ Sectional view through the terraces.
- ◂ Crisp limestone detailing.

- The ramped path through the pool.
- The central path descends below the pool and leads outside.
- The stone details are simple and beautiful.
- View of the terraces descending to the stone-lined pool at the bottom.

Location Dublin (IRE)

Father Collins Park

Programme Urban park for
Dublin's northern expansion
Designer Abelleyro + Romero
Architects
Client City of Dublin
Area 22 ha
Design period 2003
Implementation period
to be determined
Cost € 12,000,000

1 Sports centre	10 Running track (8 lane, 400m)
2 Future sports hall	11 Junior pitch
3 Car parking	12 Amphitheatre
4 Multi-purpose sports area	13 Aerobics circuit
5 Boulevard	14 Services
6 The ribbon	15 Recreation area
7 Rock gardens	16 Children's play area
8 Camogie pitch (camogie is womens' hurling)	17 Maintenance area
9 Soccer	

Northern Dublin has traditionally been the poor side of the city, with deprived 20th century council estates. This project is part of an attempt to change that. A competition was held as part of the northern expansion of Dublin's "North Fringe", which aims to develop some 7000 homes and nearly a million square metres of mixed use close to Dublin airport. Its brief called for a park providing active and passive recreation facilities, subject to consultation with local residents' groups and existing sports clubs. Abelleyro + Romero, who are based in Buenos Aires won the competition in November 2003.

The existing Father Collins Park in Donaghmede was laid out as sports grounds in the 1970s. The New Grange housing estate lies to the south and the Hole in the Wall Road is a straight boundary on the west. To the north is the River Mayne, and the Irish Sea is not far to the east. The existing park is largely featureless except for a sports centre, a sewage treatment plant on the northern end and some lines of field hedgerow trees.

The winning design incorporates many sports facilities, football pitches, a running track, amphitheatre and a new sports hall. There is a main boulevard, from east to west which links the main centres including both the existing and proposed sports facilities and it extends beyond the park to the new development areas. This boulevard is to be lined with lime trees (*Tilia platyphillos*) with an outer row of oak (*Quercus robur*). There is also a north-south axis described as a "concrete ribbon", which is the spine of the park. The concrete ribbon rises over the boulevard, and bridges the new sports hall and also passes across a central formal lake termed a "water mirror". To the south is a large multi-purpose sports

⚘ A main entrance.
⚘ Play areas are dispersed throughout the park.
⚘ Water mirror.

- Night-time view. Note how the east-west boulevard on the left extends beyond the park and links the park with the new housing.
- An aerobics station at night.
- The boulevard.

pitch and car parks on either side of the sports centre. Football pitches are located on the northern and western sides of the park and are enfolded by perimeter woodland planting.

The "ribbon" leads to an amphitheatre, for cultural displays, which lies at the head of the lake. The lake is intended for active boating and kayaking with inlets and quays built into the concrete ribbon, which rises and falls like a concrete wave to form buildings and structures. There are, in addition, a range of other sports facilities: an aerobic circuit, a running track, and play areas as well as a rock garden. Encircling all these uses is the perimeter woodland planting.

At first glance the forms are similar to Latitude Nord's Riem Park in Munich (see page 196), the situation at the edge of a city is comparable, and both are part of wider urban expansion schemes. But Abelleyro + Romero's park design is an active sports park and is more enclosed. It has a strong design philosophy of sustainability, aiming for low maintenance requirements and using low-cost materials: concrete structures with some stone paving. There is also a symbolic storyline with representations of the elements of water, air and stone: water in the formal axial lake, air in the form of a line of windmills which are intended to make the park self-sufficient in energy and a geological display in the rock garden. The park has an educational intent.

Light-leaved rows of trees, like the limes along the boulevard and rows of white poplar (*Populus alba*) and *Acacia cyanophyllla*, are intended to contrast with dark green conifers such as Scots Pine (*Pinus sylvestris*) and *Cupressocyparis leylandii* and the autumnal reds of the exotic Mexican swamp cypress (*Taxodium mucronatum*). Conifers are to be planted in the north west, while the main blocks of the perimeter woodland grove are of deciduous broad-leaved trees, to ensure maximum penetration of the sun in winter. The perimeter grove planting is also intended to be clipped in a formal way and side-trimmed.

The jury commented on the significance of the concept. "To raise the value of the area the concept of open-space-first pump-priming development is very important." This is a very significant competition and after two years of discussion is the project now likely to be built.

↕   This is a sports park to be used by night and day.
▾ | ▴ Play areas are dispersed throughout the park.

Location Enschede (NL)

Van Heekplein market square

Programme Market square
redevelopment
Designer OKRA
Landschapsarchitecten
Client municipality of Enschede
Area 1.3 ha
Design period 1999–2001
Implementation period
2002–2003
Cost € 2,500,000

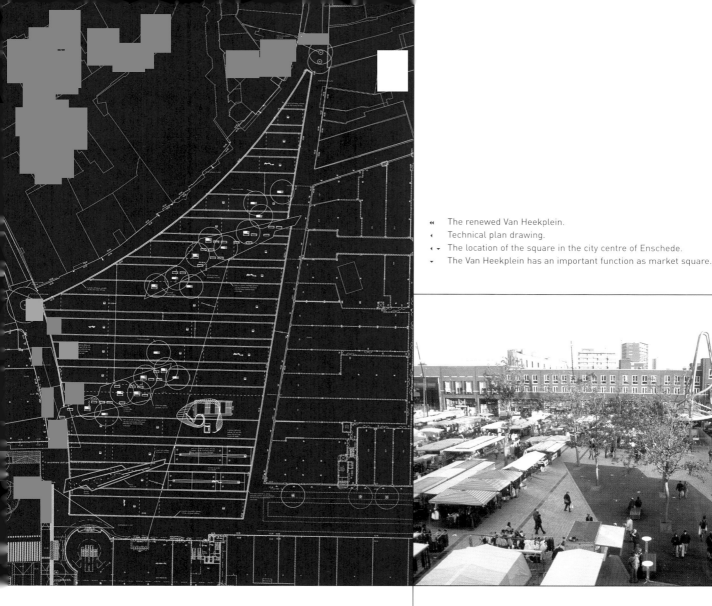

« The renewed Van Heekplein.
‹ Technical plan drawing.
‹ ▾ The location of the square in the city centre of Enschede.
▾ The Van Heekplein has an important function as market square.

Squares are the prime open spaces in towns and cities. They provide circulation space and public amenity space and function as marketplace and stage. But squares are facing increasingly difficult times. Through traffic is increasingly diverted away from town centres on ring roads. In the worst cases, occasionally a few people will gather in a square, only to quickly disperse again. And each square now has to compete with the many others in the city to host public events and performances.

This was the fate of Van Heekplein to the south of Enschede city centre. The construction of a four-lane road through the city cut the square off from the city centre, turning it into an isolated and unattractive place to visit. In recent years it had become merely a car park. As a square it was no match for the more convivial atmosphere of the Oude Markt, with its cafés and church, the dynamic Stationsplein and the intimate atmosphere of the square in front of the town hall. The only highlight was the weekly market.

The city council responded to this situation by deciding to transform the Van Heekplein into a high quality urban space. OKRA Landschaps-architecten in Utrecht drew up the design for the square as an elaboration of the urban plan for the whole area by West 8 Landscape architects.

In the new square the parking facilities have been moved underground. The focus of the square is still the market and the surrounding department stores and shops. But even when the shops are shut and the market is over, Van Heekplein should still invite people to linger awhile. OKRA distinguishes between three moments: the square in daytime, the square as market place and the square at night.

▴   Trees have been relocated to form clusters.
▸   The movable benches.

Van Heekplein is spacious comparable with the Vrijthof in Maastricht and the Dam in Amsterdam. To break up this endless space, the existing plane trees have been relocated to form two clusters. The surfacing consists of grey granite slabs with hidden drains and tree grilles around the plane trees. Two benches have been provided which can be moved around the square and used as podiums. These bench-podiums can be fixed to the ground in small holes in the surface of the square. On the south side of the square a mist fountain has been installed in an asphalted area with gratings. The fountain is computer-controlled: it produces a cloud of mist when there is little wind and jets of water in windy weather.

OKRA also made a design for the market. They created a number of main and side aisles by placing the stalls further apart or closer together. The stall layout creates meeting places and intimate areas where the paths cross and in left-over corners. The market has been given themed areas, from fruit and vegetables to cheese and from flowers to fish (the fish market has an asphalt surface with drainage gutters). In the evening the square is lit as if it were a stage set. Depending on the activity, the individual lighting elements can be turned on or off.

The selection committee was delighted to see how the designers succeeded in bringing a difficult commission to a successful conclusion. Many towns and cities are wrestling with the problem of empty squares that have no function at all outside market hours. Van Heekplein is a positive example of how to design a flexible urban space that also provides a stable environment for regular visitors.

Location Esplugues de Llobregat (E)

Torrent d'en Farré public park

Programme Public park in
a former gully
Designer Isabel Bennasar
Félix, MMAMB
Client municipality of
Esplugues de Llobregat
Area 12 ha
Design period 2000-2002
Implementation period
2001-2004
Cost € 7,121,520

The carefully situated and skilfully composed new parks and squares of Barcelona are examples to us all. Such a park can also be found in the neighbouring municipality of Esplugues de Llobregat to the west of the city. The municipal authority decided to transform the centrally located erosion gully into a municipal park. After the drainage channel was canalised and rerouted, the gully lost its discharge function, and for decades it wound its way through the town like an impenetrable and inhospitable green wasteland; gravel and clay were extracted and waste dumped in it – until its potential was discovered.

The dry gully runs for more than one and a half kilometres and has two narrow upstream forks to the north and a wider downstream stretch to the south. The plans for these three areas have now been completed. The section linking the north and south still has a neglected appearance and is bisected by the bend of a road. Once the road has been straightened it will be the final section to be landscaped. The result will be an unusual and attractive municipal park. Designer Isabel Bennasar designed the gully as an entity. The planning process began with defining a number of "unifying elements" and much attention was paid to transforming the bottom of the gully into a green promenade. A pathway marked by a regular pattern of timber sleepers set into the grass runs through all the different areas in the park. Informal links have been created between the path at the bottom of the park and the residential neighbourhoods higher up. Where possible, entrances and passageways organically join the park to the streets and alleys of the town. Existing vegetation on the steep slopes has been retained where possible, and occasionally strengthened with additional planting, heightening the

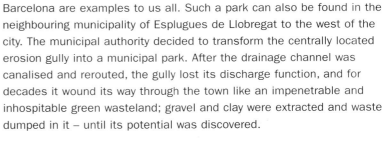
View of the inside of one of the branches. (Photo: Aleix Baguél
The masterplan for the park development. Three parts can be distinguished, main area with the pond and two branches on the north.
Original state of the dry gully.

impression of a low-lying enclosed park. The park facilities are located on plateaus on the edge of the gully, suitably integrated into the surrounding vegetation but this natural appearance is subtly corrected by the built elements. Beams, decking, retaining walls and plateaus have been used to alter the original contours to create a more stylised appearance, or as the designer calls it, "geometrised".

This controlled manipulation and cultivation of nature is what the jury finds so pleasing in the park. The designers have transformed a "non-site" into a recognizable and wonderfully diverse space within the town. The atmosphere in the northern arms of the gully, which connect it to the old town, is intimate: a narrow gully, an angled decking path, benches, bottom lighting and tree clusters. The wider dimensions of the southern part provided ample room for the construction of several facilities. The gully's hydrological past has been reflected in an elongated pond set into the relief at three levels, which gives the park a centre. Next to it are several playing fields. The bar and terraces have been strategically incorporated into the steps to the bridge that spans the entire park.

CAN HOSPITAL
1st PHASE

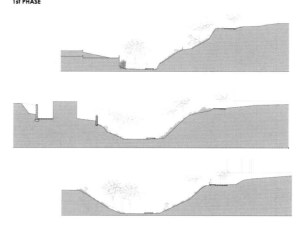

CAN CASANOVES
2nd PHASE

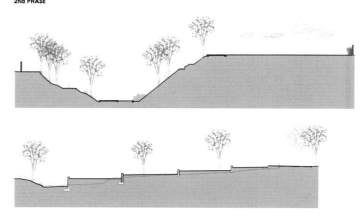

TORRENT D'EN FARRÉ
3rd PHASE

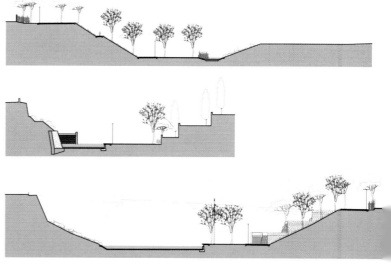

- ‹‹ ▴ Central linear path and access path from one of the slopes.
- ‹ ▴ Terracing the topography, forming playgrounds and fields.
- ▴ Intimate atmosphere in the northern arms of the gully. (Photos: Aleix Bagué)
- ‹ Sequence of cross sections through the whole park. Gradually widening topography, careful treatment of existing tree vegetation.
- ‹‹ ▾ View of the central area and the pond. The park constitutes literally a new level of urban life.
- ▸ View of the park. The foundation of the new bridge on the left serves as a bar.
- ▾ Acces path from :he park.

St Niklaus Garden of Remembrance

Programme Memorial for
urns of cremation ashes
Designer Toni Weber, w+s
Landschaftsarchitekten BSLA
Client Catholic church
community of St Niklaus,
Rüttenen, Riedholz and
Feldbrunnen
Area 630 m²
Design period 2001
Implementation period 2001
Cost € 57,900

Sometimes there is more meaning in simplicity. This is a design for a communal memorial for urns of cremation ashes within an existing cemetery. It lies between two paths in the eastern part of the cemetery and is enclosed by formal clipped hedges on three sides. Within this small and simple space lies an austere rectangular lawn 19 by 8 metres, set within wide gravel margins and planted to form a carpet of *Scilla* and white *Crocus* in spring. The space is marked by a linear pool of steel set orthogonally and asymmetrically across the rectangle. The linear pool creates a horizontal line; the lawn slopes down 15 centimetres from the level of the pool to the end of the garden.

At one end of the space, set asymmetrically away from the linear pool is a simple, rectangular stone sculptural cube of 300 black basalt stones, each 24 by 12 by 12 centimetres. This cube is surrounded by a reflective steel mirror pool 2.5 metres square and slightly raised above the ground. There is space in the lawn for 300 cremation urns to be buried. At each funeral a basalt block will be taken from the stone sculpture, carved with the name and dates of the deceased and placed in the long pool. Over the years this will gradually fill with stones of remembrance. As the linear pool fills it will become a ribbon of remembrance, and the sculpture of stone will have been removed leaving a square basin.

◄   Lawn, long pool, and the memorial stones filling it create a remembrance in time.
▲   A design of great simplicity and tranquillity.
(All photos: Pascal Hegner)

BEATRICE
STADLER-WELTI
1941 — 2002

HANS-UELI
MEISTER
1949 — 2002

HANNY BOILLAT
HERRMANN
1920 — 2002

ELISABETH
STUDER-URBEN
1929 — 2002

HANS
SCHÄREN
1928 — 2002

MARGRIT
SCHNEIDER
-KUPFER
1926 — 2002

URS
HAMMER
1928 — 2002

MYRTHA PFISTER
STAMPFLI
1918 — 2000

HANS
KIENER
1929 — 2001

HANS
WIELAND
1923 — 2001

HERMANN
BETTSCHEN
1911 — 2002

WERNER
VON BÜREN
1912 — 2001

- The long pool merges with the grass as do the ashes of the deceased.
- Set within an existing cemetery, this garden is an area of communal remembrance; 12 cubic stones had been removed during 2001 and 2002 to form memorials.
- The cube is made up 300 cubic blocks of basalt, which are removed one by one, engraved and then placed in the long pool.

- A plan remarkable for its "functionality, strength, and simplicity".
- The pool is formed in rusting steel which itself is changing.

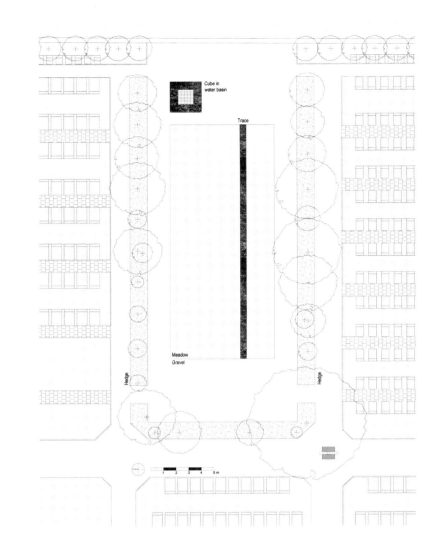

This is a design of exquisite and yet appropriate simplicity. Water is a symbol of life and the cube is the symbol of community. Together they form a composition for the remembrance of the lives lived in this community.

The jury remarked that the design was distinguished by its qualities of "functionality, strength, and simplicity". This design may be simple, but it is full of meaning and creates a place of memory. Remembrance is both personal but also communal in that the process of the passing of lives lived within a small community will be marked as the stones move.

Rottenrow Gardens

Programme Transformation
of former hospital grounds
into a public garden
Designer GROSS.MAX
Landscape Architects
Client Strathclyde University
Area 1 ha
Design period 2002-2003
Implementation period 2003
Cost € 1,059,650

GROSS.MAX have transformed the sloping site of the former Royal Maternity Hospital (1860 to 2001) on Rottenrow into gardens that form a centre for the University of Strathclyde's campus. The designers aimed "to unravel the historic layers of the site not unlike a sensuous act of urban striptease". So elements of the old Maternity Hospital such as the Rottenrow portico, the North Portland Street arch and a series of white glazed brick retaining walls have been retained. The designers then created terraced gardens with, as a central core, a wide flight of concrete steps that bridge an eight-metre height level difference so that the steps can also act as informal seating and a performance area. The south facing slopes of the gardens have been terraced into a series of viewing platforms overlooking the garden and the Glasgow skyline beyond.

- Digital plan.
- Aerial view showing the gardens with Glaswegians sunbathing; the gardens are set amidst the buildings of the University of Strathclyde and create a central place for the relatively new (forty-year old) university.
- The pool below.

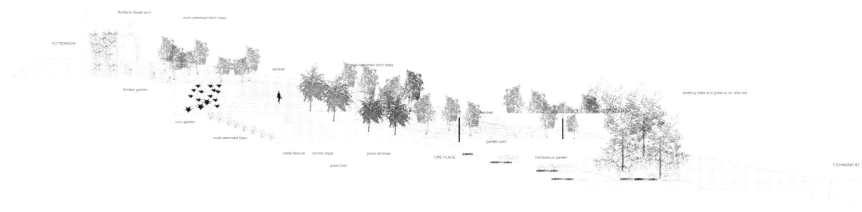

The highest terrace is lined with a wisteria-covered (*Wisteria sinensis*) pergola, low concrete retaining walls and 1.2 metre-high beech hedges. A footpath alongside the three metre high gabion retaining wall leads to a lower level look-out planted with a solitary ash tree (*Fraxinus excelsior*). From here water spouts to a pool below. The gabion baskets are filled with crushed sandstone salvaged from the demolished hospital building. Below is a rock garden with large pieces of salvaged stonework, planted with a mixture of Gunnera (*Gunnera giganteum*), Lily (*Lilium giganteum*) and ferns (*Dyopteris filix-mas*). In contrast to the linearity of the south facing terraced gardens, the easterly slopes of the garden are contoured in voluptuous mounds planted with ornamental grasses, ivy and birch (*Betula jacquemontii*). A sweeping, ramped footpath descends through the mounded earth to the lower level of the garden. The lower level centre of the garden consists of a limestone-paved square, raised water feature and lawn or to use the Scots, a pleasance, planted with snowdrops (the emblem of the former hospital), and a willow-planted (*Salix spp*) embankment. From here the site continues in a terraced herbaceous garden planted with blocks of lilies, geraniums (*Geranium sanguineum*), lavender (*Lavandula angustifolia 'Hidcote'*) and red hot pokers (*Kniphofia*). Rows of crab apple (*Malus domestica*) transect this garden. Seating areas allow the visitor to overlook the wetland and wild flower meadow located below in the garden's south westerly corner.

The jury felt that this scheme was remarkable for "its density of contextualism, it is well designed and well made, modern without being overpretentious… it exploits the topography, incorporates existing old stone arches into the park area and has a well integrated balance between gardens, open space and plazas". It is also a very rich addition to Glasgow's city scene. Eelco Hooftman from GROSS MAX comments that "most buildings destroy landscape; for once to destroy a building in order to create a landscape feels like sweet revenge".

‹‹ Sectional elevation north-south.

‹ The gardens as a public gathering: opening day in 2004.

▾ GROSS.MAX design image.

‹ ▴ South-facing terraces create suntraps for talk.

‹ Hills clad in ivy and multi-stemmed birch lie to the right of the grand steps and the hubbub of the city is disguised by the bubble of the fountains.

▸ The stones for the gabion retaining walls come from the demolished Rottenrow Hospital.

▾ The garden.

139

Farmyards in Hogeland

Programme Design and
construction regulation
guidelines for extension
and renovation of existing
farmyards
Designer Veenenbos en Bosch
Landschapsarchitecten
Client Libau Provincial Building
Commission
Area 55,000 ha
Design period 2002-2003
Implementation period
2004 onward
Cost to be determined

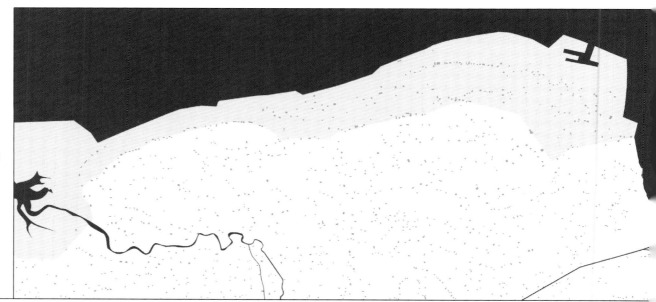

Hogeland, an area of polders and terp landscape along the northern fringe of the Netherlands, is a unique piece of landscape heritage. The area was gradually won from the sea over hundreds of years and arable farming prospered on the rich clay soils. The landscape is dominated by the vast scale of the open space, relieved by subtle natural curves and criss-crossed by wet and dry creeks, dikes and transparent rows of trees. The monumental farmhouses stand like sentinels on the horizon. This seemingly timeless and irreplaceable topography is threatened by the force of international agricultural policy, agricultural legislation and autonomous processes. The attractive, leafy old farmyards cannot resist the pressures of the increasing scale of production and farm diversification, while new agro-industrial enterprises and farm conversions erode the traditional functional relationship between the farmyard buildings and planting and farming practice.

Veenenbos en Bosch Landschapsarchitecten has devised a solution to this problem. They have introduced a new prototype farmyard for Hogeland that does justice to the historic features of the area and at the same time meet the needs of the modern farm. It consists of a set of spatial and administrative rules, kept as simple, flexible and repeatable as possible to promote their uniform application across the whole

‹ A rural landscape. Distribution of individual farmsteads in the north-eastern part of the Netherlands.
‹ ◄ Richly planted farmsteads in the Hogeland region are like islands in the polder landscape.
◄ Proposed development scheme for an existing farm. Reconstruction of the old yard, osier bed, three individual homes.

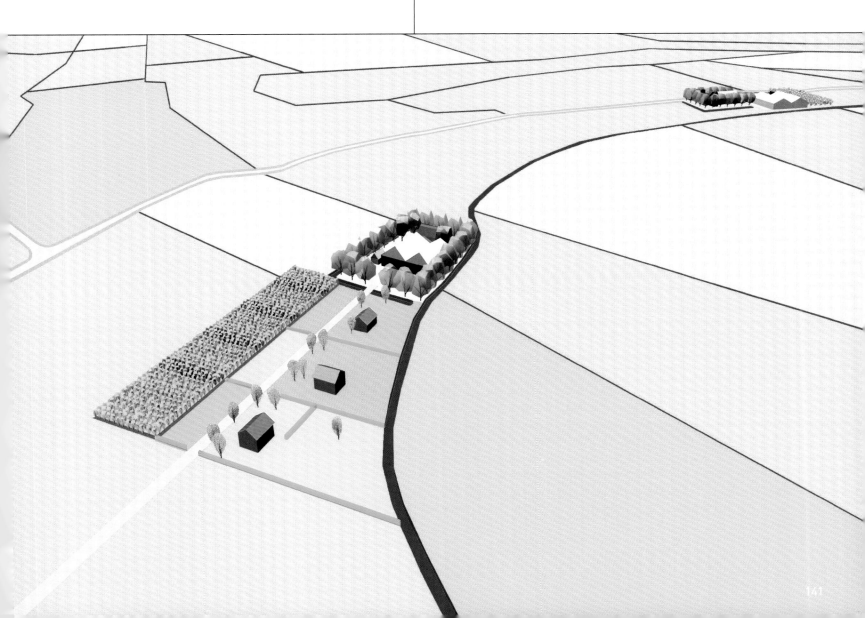

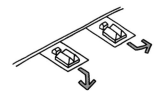

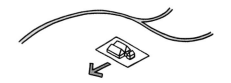

Farmstead extension criteria.
- Extension away from neighbouring farmhouses. Extension away from roads and paths. Extensions away from historic patterns and objects.
‣ Extension of sprout farm. Reconstruction of old farmhouse, double volume of barn, wind turbine and woodland.

landscape. The prescriptions cover the direction and size of any expansion of farmyards, the colour of new barns and livestock sheds and treatment of the existing farmyard. They also require that at least a third of any farmyard extension is planted. A crucial element in the prototype is the opportunity for owners to sell a proportion of the farmyard plot for new housing when they stop farming. This prevents uncontrolled expansion of new homes in the sensitive landscape and offers farmers alternative economic prospects. These development rights, acquired if the farmyard extension conforms to the guidelines, are transferable to new owners of the farm, but may not be transferred to another site.

The designers have brought to life and tested the prototype in master plans for two existing farmyards. The first plan is for a livestock farm in the terp landscape. The farmyard was extended to the south, and after the farm closes there is room for at most three new homes. The second plan is for a sprout farmer in the polder and dike landscape. His extension involves doubling the area of sheds and the planting of a wooded pasture, which earns him the right to erect a wind turbine.

The jury believes that the farmyard project involves citizens, politicians and professionals in a realistic and instructive manner in the rapid changes taking place in the rural landscape. The design study alerts us to the urgency of the problem and the importance of a professional approach to historic values on a regional scale. In their professional simulations the designers show that in a protected landscape time does not have to stand still.

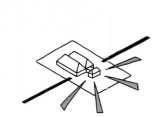

Farmstead development criteria.
- View towards and from the old farmhouse continued; extension should be connected.
‣ Extension plot is autonomous from the original plot; future extension direction is indicated. On third of extension plot to be planted with one type of vegetation. In case of farm closure, maximum of three new homes allowed, minimum building plot 1500 square meters. Careful reconstruction of old farmsteads: ditch, garden, tall trees.
  New sheds and barns one colour; wind turbine is possible.
  Four types of green within the plot: orchard, woodland, forest, osier bed.

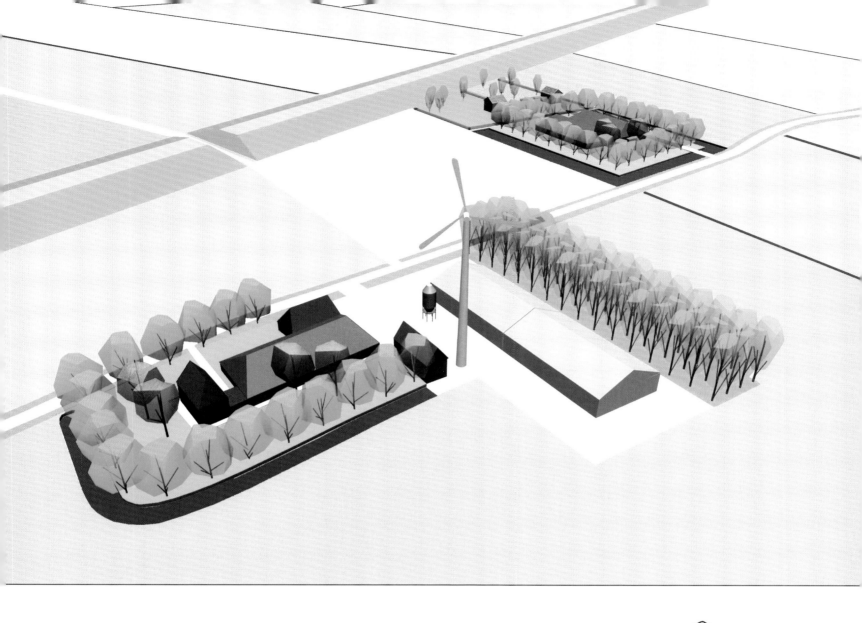

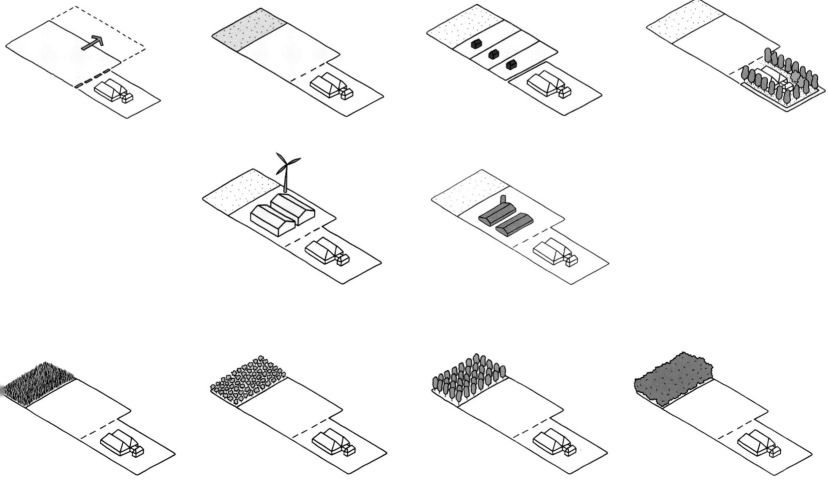

Holland's Green Heart

Programme Management
and development tools for
sustainable landscape
conservation
Designer H+N+S
Landschapsarchitecten
In collaboration with
ABF Research
Client Provinces of North
Holland, South Holland
and Utrecht
Area 180,000 ha
Design period 2002-2004

Implementation period
it acts as a vision and basis
for further projects
Cost to be determined

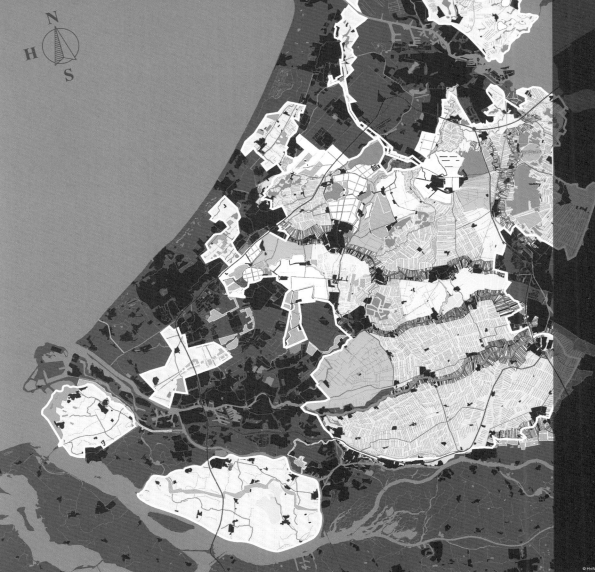

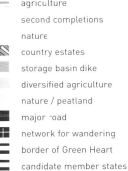

Programme

/ / / agriculture

diversified agriculture

nature

agriculture

second completions

nature

country estates

storage basin dike

diversified agriculture

nature / peatland

major road

network for wandering

border of Green Heart

candidate member states

t was a brilliant idea. A little under 40 years ago the large polder and water landscape enclosed by the Amsterdam, Leiden, Rotterdam and Utrecht conurbations was named the 'Green Heart'. No other Dutch planning concept has been as successful as this simple designation of a patchwork landscape of farmland, nature reserves, lakes and villages. It is undoubtedly the reason why in every policy update since then, national and provincial planners have simply been able to redraw the boundary of the Green Heart and formulate several impassioned statements on protecting the area against urban development.

The regional plan for the future of the Green Heart by H+N+S Landschapsarchitecten is the first comprehensive manifesto that provides tools for expressing the concept and gives it a topography and a strategy. Despite its sacrosanct status, the Green Heart is under threat, from outside pressures and from within. The designers have not closed their eyes to these: a continuing stream of small house-building projects, the criss-crossing infrastructure, mineralization of the flat, peaty soils, insufficient capacity for storing surface water and a rapid worsening of the prospects for farming. The underlying aim of the plan is to create a bond between the urban population of the Randstad and the qualities and potential of the Green Heart that reflects contemporary life. The main spatial development proposals are described in three chapters: the renewal of the water system; the radical improvement in access for the urban population; and selective, high-quality suburban development.

The water system will be renovated in two ways. To ensure the long-term conservation of the lowland peat soils, the water table in the former

▲ Master plan for Holland's Green Heart. Development of a fruitful relationship between town and countryside.

◄ Urban development along the boundaries of the Green Heart. (Photo: Peter van Bolhuis, Pandion)

agricultural grasslands will be raised considerably. The resulting bogs and lakes can be bought and managed by various nature conservation organizations (privately by individuals or bodies; publicly by one or more organizations). Where this is not necessary or possible, additional water storage capacity has been created in the form of a chain of water storage fields enclosed by dikes for the temporary retention of excess precipitation. This storage basin will also form a brand new regional ecological and recreational backbone. The creation of a fine network of cycleways and footpaths will open up the landscape to the public and support efforts by farmers in the Green Heart to develop local markets. The last proposal is for housing projects that make a positive contribution to the landscape. In secure, selected zones, living environments can be developed that complement the supply of urban housing; the additional returns they generate will be invested in extra space for the water storage basin or in new collectively managed natural habitats.

Regional landscape architecture with a strong hydrological, ecological and planning input is not easy to judge. It took the jury some considerable time and much discussion before they realized the full relevance and intelligence of the design. The plan for the Green Heart is a contagious, 21st century resumption of an age-old Dutch tradition of utilitarian landscape development on a regional scale.

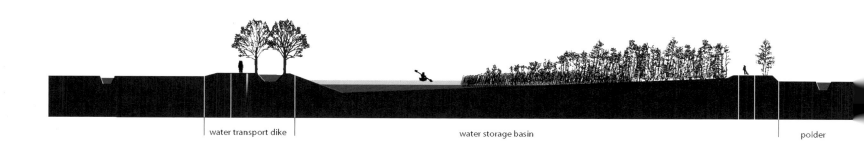

water transport dike   water storage basin   polder

| ▸ Assembled aerial view of the water storage fields. After a dry period (top) and a period of heavy rainfall (below). (Photos: Paul Paris)

The New Gardens in the Dyck Field

Programme Public park
with theme gardens at the
Centre for Garden design
and Landscape Culture at
Schloss Dyck
Designer RMP
Landschaftsarchitekten
Client Schloss Dyck Foundation
Area 30 ha
Design period 2000-2001
Implementation period
2001-2002
Cost € 7,500,000

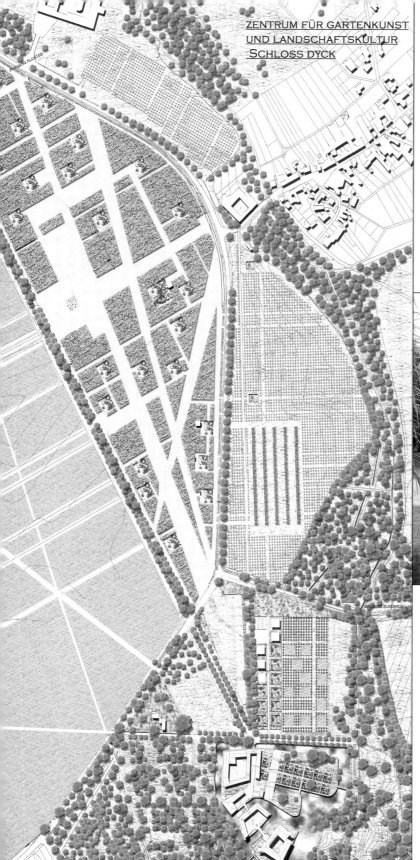

| ▲ Situation of the New Gardens in front of Schloss Dyck (seen at the bottom of the plan, and in the background in the aerial view).
The New Gardens are a field and a park at the same time. (Photo: Hans Dijkstra, bvBeeld)

Schloss Dyck is located on the flatlands on the left side of the Rhine near Düsseldorf. In terms of cultural history, the castle and grounds are among the most important in the Rhineland. A private foundation and public funds are currently turning the property into a Centre for Garden Design and Landscape Culture. The moated Baroque castle is undergoing expensive restorations until 2008; the first parts of the building to be completed have been open since 2003. The castle is surrounded by a historic English-style castle park with a remarkable collection of rare tree species. It was designed mainly by the Scottish landscape architect Thomas Blaikie, with the collaboration of the German landscape designers Peter Joseph Lenné and Maximilian Friedrich Weyhe.

Complementing the castle park is contemporary work by Stephan Lenzen of RMP Landscape Architects. In 2000, he won the design competition for the New Gardens in the Dyck Field, held in preparation for the Decentralised State Garden Show in 2002, on which occasion the federal state of North Rhine-Westphalia restored seven historic parks and gardens along the Lower Rhine. The New Gardens in the Dyck Field were the only "new architecture" in this garden show. As their name suggests, they consist of several theme gardens incorporated in one large field – that is, in farmland.

This astoundingly simple concept and its spatial realization won over the jury of the present publication. Not only were the theme gardens integrated into a field which is in use agriculturally and yet nevertheless formally designed but also the landscape architect succeeded in putting through this "field design" as the leitmotiv for a garden show.

A considerable achievement. The jurors virtually envied the originator for the subtle finesse of the formal design with materials that are not formal at all.

In fact, to define Dyck Field, Lenzen works mainly with one material: giant Chinese silver grass (*Miscanthus 'Giganteus'*). In the 1930's, miscanthus was considered a botanical innovation; coming from Denmark, it spread to German ornamental gardens as a structuring and yet filigree solitaire. Moreover, miscanthus is a useful plant marketed as a source of bio energy and as insulation material. At Dyck Field the landscape architects wanted to give this economic value back to their material – hence the miscanthus crop is grown, harvested and brought to market just like the corn from the fields all around.

They designed the field to be a park at the same time. It is based on the historic chestnut avenue; the old trees provide it with structure and form the backdrop for the 24 theme gardens that appear like actors on the field-stage. The stage itself is variable. After the giant Chinese silver grass harvest in spring, the theme gardens form positive spatial masses rising up out of the low field. The visitor's gaze sweeps across the broad farmland landscape. In the course of the seasons, the miscanthus grows up to four metres tall and the gardens "sink" into the sea of grasses. Visitors dip in and wander at will between the miscanthus masses rustling in the wind. The garden spaces are always a surprise when they open up in the swaying jungle labyrinth. The landscape architects use spacious lawn passages to keep lanes free and afford view corridors from the castle to the Saint Nikolaus monastery and the Dyck wine tavern.

↑ Miscanthus Giganteus is grown in the New Gardens and harvested like the corn in the surrounding fields. (Photo: Hans Dijkstra, bvBeeld)
◆ In the course of the seasons the Miscanthus grows tall and forms a swaying labyrinth.

▲ | ▼ Sunken into the Miscanthus field there are 24 theme gardens such as Heron's Grove (above), the Agricultural Theatre (below), the field with sculptures by Ulrich Rückriem (bottom).

▲ | ▸ The theme garden "Plantwork
Orange" features reddish
materials and red flowering
plants.

pflanzwerk orange

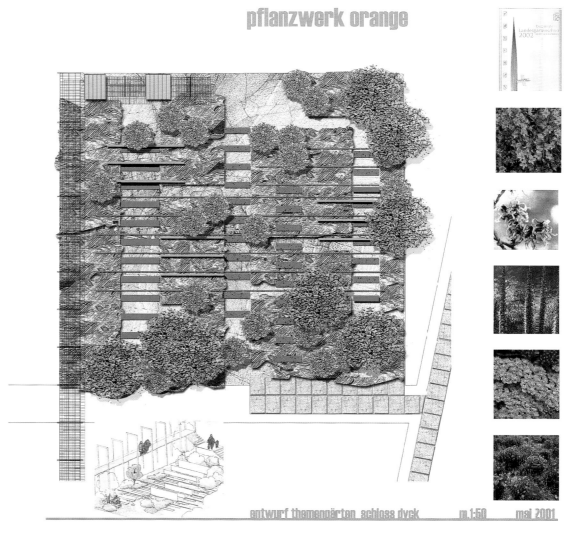

entwurf themengärten schloss dyck   m.1:50   mai 2001

entwurf themengärten_schloss dyck   m 1:50   mai 2001

RADERSCHALL BÜHRER PETERS LENZEN
RMP

◄ | ▾ The "White Garden" at
the Dyck Field.

Strips of 1.50-metre-wide slate-coloured concrete flagstones along the lanes guide visitors through the "Agricultural Park".

Stephan Lenzen designed 14 theme gardens according to free associations, such as "Bed in the Cornfield", "Heron's Grove", "Judaic Garden", "Blue Garden" and "Plantwork Orange". Eight other gardens were shaped by well-known landscape designers; two served as testing ground for the next generation (see page 154, "Cargo Garden").

Cargo Garden

Programme Theme garden
in the park at the centre for
Garden Design and Landscape
Culture at Schloss Dyck
Designer relais
Landschaftsarchitekten
Client Schloss Dyck Foundation
Area 625 m²
Design period 2001-2002
Implementation period 2002
Cost € 35,000

Cargo is the name of this theme garden. It is about freight. Right in the middle of the monoculture of giant Chinese silver grass in the Dyck Castle Park, relais Landschaftsarchitekten unload a shipment of plants. As though exploding with their modulations, splendid colours and exoticism, the plants create a new world in a minimum of space. A Big Bang in the universe of a ploughed field.

In 2001, the Berlin landscape architects won a realization competition held across Germany for the design of a theme garden among the New Gardens in the Dyck Field (see page 148), one of the seven venues of the Decentralised State Garden Show in 2002 in North Rhine-Westphalia. The site was a square field measuring 25 by 25 metres in the silver-grass sea of the park. The planners enclosed this square in a wooden frame. Nine wooden ribs trace parallel strips into it; they could be rails in a shunting station. All around the edge, wooden planks form a deck: a gangway for stevedores, a sundeck for garden travellers. Benches made of wooden planks on one side recall Euro-palettes and invite visitors to stay a while – until the freight is loaded and the voyage begins.

The landscape architects poured crushed basalt stone and planted clusters of vegetation in alternating parallel strips. The same proximity of stone and plants can be found between real railway tracks. Only the planners did not leave the selection of plants up to the wind, weather and migrating birds. Instead, they defined exactly two vegetation modules, whose appearance differs clearly as to height, form and colours of the leaves and flowers. The fennel and white gaura module (Foeniculum-Gaura) forms delicately veined, whitish pink cushions of vegetation, with long-stemmed poppies and allium heads arising from them. In contrast, the palma Christi module (Ricinus) features the spread of dark palma Christi leaves, as big as the palm of a hand and occupying a lot of space,

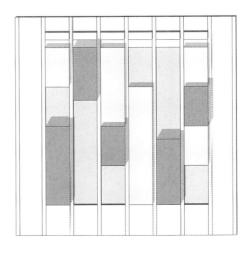

with colourful tulip and iris hybrids flourishing among them. The landscape architects harmonized the species and varieties with great finesse. They were free and easy about combining plants of the widest variety of origins – exotic and indigenous, strange and natural, castor-oil plant and daisies joining in unusual neighbourly relations.

At a distance, the jury was hesitant at first: was this a lifestyle garden or an especially sensitive piece of work? Eventually the prevailing view was that this work was much too minimalist to succeed as a garden composition that aims to please. The wooden ribs are much too narrow for anyone to walk along, the crushed stone is much too barren to convey fertile soil, there is much too much of "almost nothing". While it breaks with the customary garden atmosphere, it lets a sparkling cargo of vegetation explode.

◂ View of the Cargo Garden in the freshly planted Dyck Field.

▾ The Cargo Garden sunken into the fully grown Miscanthus field.

▴ Palma Christi vegetation module "Ricinus": Tulipa hybrid 'Queen of the Night', Tulipa hybrid 'Menton', Tulipa hybrid 'Baronesse', Euphorbia pclychroma, Iris-Barbata-Elatior hybrid 'Red Orchid', Iris-Barbata-Elatior hybrid 'Dental Rose', Ricinus gibsonii. Fennel-white gaura vegetation module "Foeniculum-Gaura": Bellis perennis 'Robella', Bellis perennis 'Roggli White', Myosotis sylvestris 'Rosylva', Viola cornuta 'Sorbet Coconut', Allium 'Mount Everest', Lupinus-Polyphyllus hybrid 'La Chatelaine', Lupinus-Pclyphyllus hybrid 'My Castle', Papaver orientale 'Queen Alexandra', Salvia nemorosa 'Adrian', Dahlia hybrid 'Arabian Night', Dahlia hybrid 'Park Princess', Foeniculum vulgare 'Atropurpureum', Gaura lindheimeri.

Location Kočevje (SLO)

Grounds for Ob Rinži elementary school

Programme Grounds for
an elementary school
Designer Ana Kučan
In collaboration with
Damjan Cerne
Client municipality of Kočevje,
Slovenian Ministry of Education
Area 3.5 ha
Design period 1996-1998
Implementation period
2000-2004
Cost € 385,000

◂ ▾   Sports pitches and running tracks are also embraced by the forest.
◂   This is a school where outdoor play is in the woodland, and is not fenced off.
▾   At night the school takes on a modernist classicism framed by trees.
⚡   The school is set into woodland on the edge of Kočevje.

This is a school set in the pine forests of Kočevje, a small town of ten thousand people in southern Slovenia. It is functionally and structurally divided in two parts, one for six- to nine-year-olds and one for ten- to 14-year olds. The building is an articulated modernist structure, in concrete and wood, which is set astride the ups and downs of the karst landscape. Karst is characteristic of Slovenia and is a limestone landscape with a combination of caves and underground channels, and a consequent rough and bumpy surface where land has collapsed in the hollows below. By contrast to the building, the landscape design aims to exploit this undulating terrain and Ana Kučan has used it to create outdoor rooms and glades for sport or play. The glades are inspired by the shape of the sinkholes, they form and act as shelters and are clear independent objects, set in the matrix of the original forest, thus rendering the surrounding woodland even more primordial. The aim is to inhabit the forest while not compromising its wildness.

The forest is oak-beech woodland with a number of introduced Norway spruce (Picea abies). Plant selection was based on the existing flora and so notable specimens of oak, beech and hornbeam were kept while the spruce was removed partly to open the spaces around the school to light and partly because they were subject to bark beetle. Shrub planting then took places to form clumps, in order to provide intermittent borders and hollow spaces within which children can hide. Flower and fruit and bright autumn leaf effects were also considered, for educational purposes as well as for visual pleasure. There are simple lime-loving appropriate plants such as Viburnum opulus 'Sterile', Cornus mas, Euonymus europaeus. Roses such as Rosa rugosa and Rosa Canina were chosen and new tree-

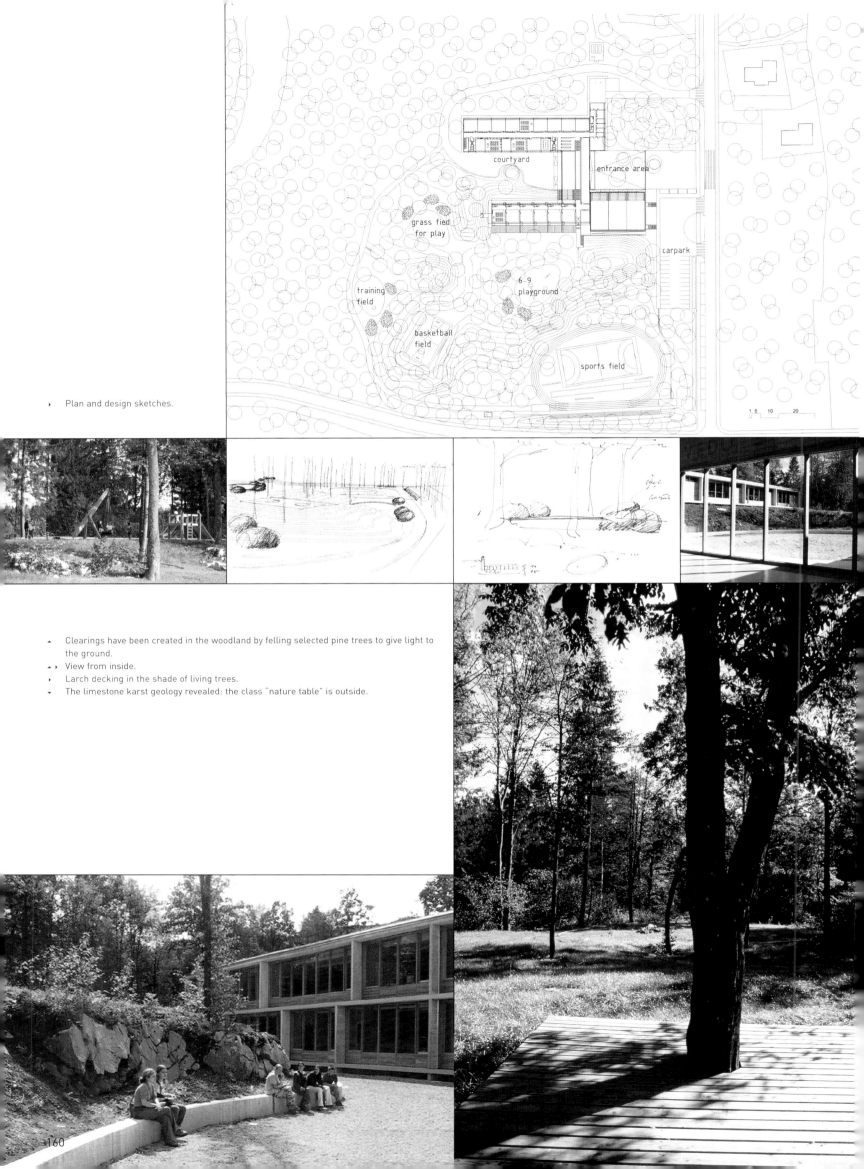

‣ Plan and design sketches.

▴ Clearings have been created in the woodland by felling selected pine trees to give light to the ground.
▴‣ View from inside.
‣ Larch decking in the shade of living trees.
▾ The limestone karst geology revealed: the class "nature table" is outside.

planting includes various *Sorbus* species. Hornbeam hedges were used to divide the outdoor classroom spaces for the youngest children (the six to nine year olds).

Due to cost constraints, paving and materials are cheap and simple, asphalt for the sports areas and paths, synthetic sports paving for the sports court, pre-cast concrete benches with larch timber seats, pre-cast concrete slabs for woodland paths and, outside building entrances, sand for cycle "slow down" areas for cycles and motorbikes. Larch on oak beams is used for the decking for the outdoor classrooms for the youngest.

It took a while to get the management right; the maintenance staff were used to concrete-paved schoolyards and car parks. Now the school maintenance staff cut the grass, look after the sand areas, clean the gutters and remove snow (salting is not permitted) while the State Forestry Department looks after the woodland areas and a professional gardener comes once a year to look after the shrub planting. The aim is to produce a rich and stimulating series of outdoor spaces, allowing both sports and active play as well as spaces that can be made the children's own, where they can release frustration and grow ties of friendship.

▸ ▲ Outdoor spaces in the woods.
▸ | ▸ The classrooms are set in the woodland. This is a school in a natural environment.

Location København (DK)

Bertel Thorvaldsens Plads

Programme Redesign
of a square with a pool
Designer Schønherr Landskab
Client Thorvaldsens Museum
and municipality of
Copenhagen
Area 5,300 m^2
Design period 1993-2002
Implementation period 2002
Cost € 1,150,000

Christiansborg is the Danish government quarter with the parliament and government offices, the Royal Library and several museums. Slotsholmen Island (on which Christiansborg lies) is protected by a moat on three sides and is situated at the centre of the city.

On the north side of the island is a square which is bordered on one side by the baroque Manège or riding school (designed by E.D. Häusser in 1745), which is part of the extensive Christiansborg Palace. On the north side of the square is the museum devoted to the sculptor Bertel Thorvaldsen, the early 19th century neo-classicist, arguably Denmark's best known sculptor. Thorvaldsens Museum and mausoleum was designed by Michael Gottlieb Bindesbøll in 1848 in a classical style. It has a glorious yellow wash, which contrasts with the the austerely white elevation of the Manège and its green copper roofs. On the third side of the square is the Frederiksholms Canal, lined by the quayside road, Vindebrogade.

The area is an expression of the eighteenth and nineteenth centuries when the Danish kingdom was appreciably bigger and grander and the monarchy more powerful. The square was originally laid out by Bindesbøll following a plan of 1839 as a simple open space with two rows of acacia trees in front of the Manège, a sculpture and a fountain.

By the 1990s the area in front of the Thorvaldsens Museum was mainly covered by car parking with traffic along Vindebrogade, and also a side road, the Porthusgade, which ran the length of the Manège. Cars dominated everything and the place had lost its identity and become a "nowhere" space.

‣ An overall view, with the Frederikholms Canal in the foreground and its embankment road. A square, a pool and tree and glorious stately architecture make for a controlled, peaceful and careful urban composition. (Photo: Thorben Eskerod)
‹ ‣ The old situation: traffic and parking area.
‹ Thorvaldsens Museum viewed from the west in summer. (Photo: Julie Breuning)
▾ Plan: the site is on the northern side of the Christiansborg Palace, alongside Frederiksholms Canal.

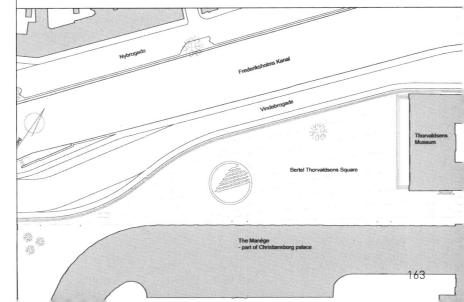

‣ Market on Thorvaldsens Square.

‣ The copper roof of the Manège on the left and Thorvaldsens Square, viewed from the roof of Thorvaldsens Museum.

‣‣ The photograph from 1870 that inspired Torben Schønherr.

The project for civilizing and celebrating the civic qualities of the space began in 1992 when the Danish Arts Foundation invited sculptor Svend Wiig Hansen to erect a sculpture in front of Thorvaldsens Museum. The Museum consequently asked landscape architect Torben Schønherr to redesign the whole square. He was inspired by the original 1839 design and by a photograph from 1870 in which, to quote critic Christopher Harlang, "...emptiness and composure are dominant elements, and the crispness of the buildings and canal bulwarks is reinforced by the simplicity that results from the black and white image". Schønherr conceived the square as a single large space with a simple surface made of cobbles. All parking places were removed. Composure, emptiness, crispness, and simplicity are also key words that can be used to describe Schønherr's design.

Svend Wiig Hansen died in 1998. A new competition led to the eventual appointment of sculptor Jørn Larsen who designed a circular reflecting pool with zig-zag patterns across it in granite setts – all at the level of the surrounding paving.

Schønherr's design for the square is the ultimate in its simplicity: consisting simply of granite setts, which march up to the enclosing buildings with one existing tree, an acacia. The plaza has been given back its space. The buildings have a suitable setting and the car no longer dominates.

▲ Emptiness and composure provide a space for the buildings, here Jørn Larsen's circular pool with E.D. Häusser's Manège of 1745.
▼ Jørn Larsen's circular pool in the winter.
(Photos: Thorben Eskerod)

Location København (DK)

Prags Boulevard

Programme Regeneration of
a mainroad into a boulevard
Designer Kristine Jensens
Tegnestue
Client municipality of
Copenhagen
Area 6.8 ha
Design period 2001-2002
Implementation period
2004-2005
Cost € 3,400,000

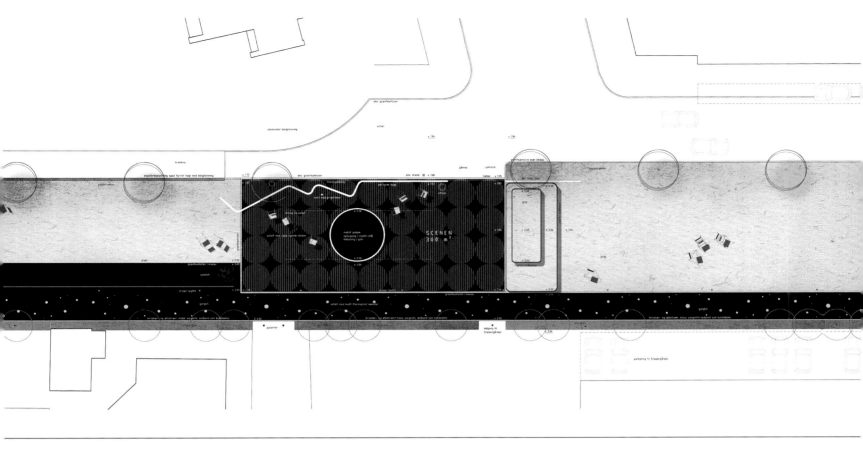

The Prags Boulevard design aims to regenerate a road in the Holmbladsgade, on Amager Island, east of central Copenhagen. Prags Boulevard itself is a straight road running eastwards through Amager to the coast. It runs through a run down area of small-scale industry and four-to five-storey housing, with a significant immigrant population, a higher level of unemployment than elsewhere in Copenhagen and a lack of smaller scale public open spaces and public gardens. The redesign of Prags Boulevard is part of the Holmbladsgade regeneration area (or Kvarterløft). It began in 2001, with a two-stage ideas competition organized by the Danish Foundation for Culture and Sports Facilities, which was won by Kristine Jensen.

Poplar trees, grass and green chairs are the three main features and the designer's aim was to compose them in a strong and striking way in order to form "clashes between the old and the hyper-modern". The new path is made in black asphalt like the road, patterned with white dots and contained by stainless-steel edging; the road kerbs are granite. The idea behind the new paving was to avoid excavation and work over the existing surfaces. Squares and activity areas are black asphalt or picked out in red paving, patterned with graphic red and white circles, and lit with green neon lights. Black rubber panels are installed, making a strong statement. The lines of poplar trees, Prags lamps and the Prags chair are the main unifying elements. White fences provide screens.

◄ The stage: a place for Tai Chi or maybe tango or meetings.

↕ Plan of the stage area which is a crossing point with Dalslandgade for both cycle- and footpaths, marked by a mobile platform and small grandstand to create a place maybe for dancing, maybe for Tai Chi, maybe for political meetings.

▲ Prags Boulevard runs across Amager Island towards the coast.

▼ This green Prags chair especially designed as a signature for the renewal. There are five elements to the design: grass, poplars, lamp, fence and this chair.

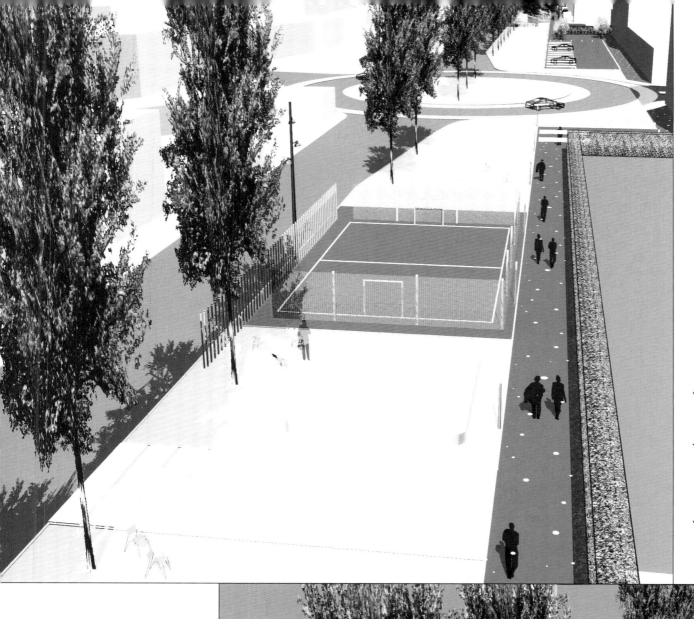

- ‹ The Cage is a sports area, with red rubberised play surface and 60 centimetre-high black rubber enclosure.
- ⌄ The Ramp is at the end of the "urban" part of Prags Boulevard where it begins to become more rural, so this is a tree-dominated place with seats, a platform and fence to screen the road.
- ‹⌄ The Prags Lamp designed for the street.

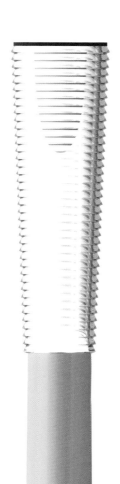

- ◄ Plan: bold use of thermoplastic paint on asphalt.
- ◄ The kindergarten: existing trees are kept, and a white fence snakes around them to create an enclosure for children with grass, and sand and soft play surfaces.

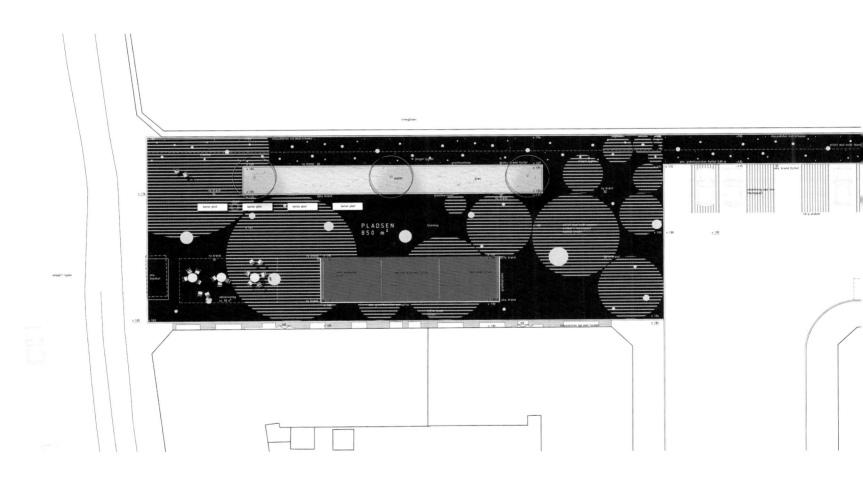

The result is a boulevard writ large, the footpaths generate a completely new atmosphere for the district. The straight line of the road is broken up by a series of new spaces along the pavement. These are organized as variations on the garden: the square, the stage, the court, cage kindergartens and areas of seating. Inner-city regeneration of declining industrial and migrant areas is a common challenge in most cities of Europe; this design sets a fresh and adventurous approach.

La Vall d'en Joan landfill landscape

Programme Restoration of
a controlled rubbish dump
Designer Battle i Roig
Arquitectes
Client Entitat Metropolitana
de Serveis Hidràulics del Àrea
Metropolitana de Barcelona,
City of Barcelona
Area 60 ha
Design period 2001-2002
Implementation period
2002-2012

170

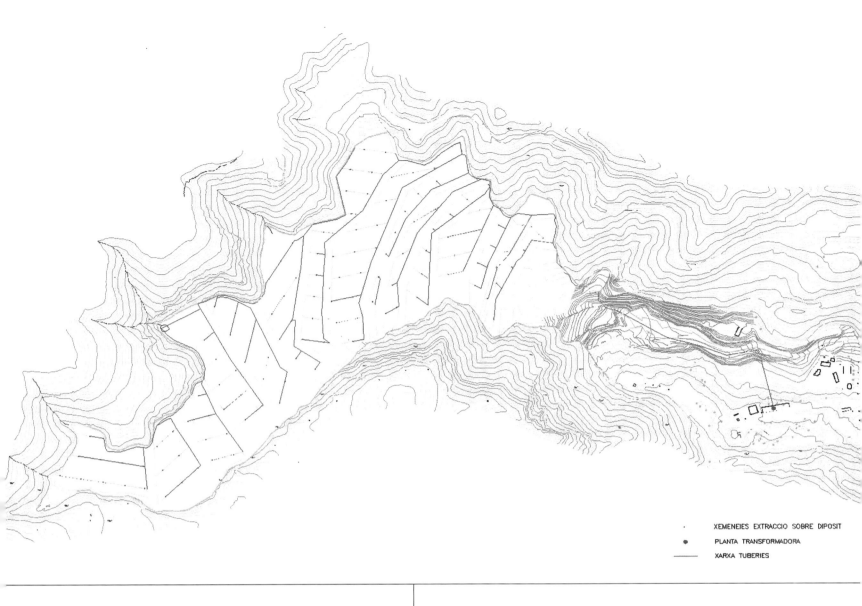

▲   Scheme of the hydrological waste-water system. Catchment, collection, purification and redistribution.

◄ ▲   The landfill before treatment and redevelopment.

◄   Aerial view of the completed situation. Terraces hold different types of agricultural vegetation. Slopes are developed naturally. Maintenance roads and footpaths zigzag up and down.
[Photos: José Hevia]

The Vall d'en Joan landfill is situated in the El Garraf massif and has been operational since 1974. The site was cleared of trees and shrubs, the landfill base was sealed with a layer of clay and a drainage system for the whole site was installed. 30 years later an enormous amount of waste has been amassed, in some places more than 80 metres deep. In a few years the landfill will reach its maximum capacity and by law must be restored. The initial design brief was to reconstruct the valley in its original state, but Battle i Roig considered this neither possible nor desirable. Building on the unique features of the site, their layout plan launched the idea of designing the valley as a public semi-agricultural landscape that reveals the local and regional ecological patterns and processes. The valley is easy to reach from the surrounding towns and villages and an international long-distance footpath passes nearby. The half-planned, half-natural transformation into a new and stable situation will take place slowly and is being closely observed.

The reconstruction of the landscape began at the lower end of the valley while at the top the landfill was still in operation. First, a new drainage system was designed to work alongside the existing system. It captures

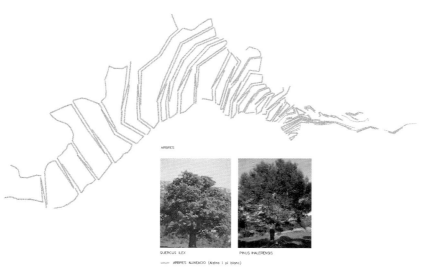

ARBRES

QUERCUS ILEX   PINUS IHALEPENSIS

▬▬ ARBRES ALINEACIO (Alzina i pi blanc)

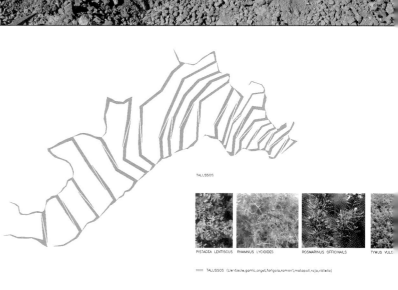

TALUSSOS

PISTACEA LENTISCUS   RHAMNUS LYCIOIDES   ROSMARINUS OFFICINAILS   TYMUS VULG

▬▬ TALUSSOS (Llentiscle,garric,arget,farigola,romani,matapoll,roja,vidiella)

BARDISSA

VIBURNUM TINUS   HEDERA HELIX   LONICERA PERYCLINELUM   LONICERA JAPONICA

▬▬ BARDISSA (Alatern,harfull,raldô,esbarzer,Arill,sl,Heura,Lligabosc)

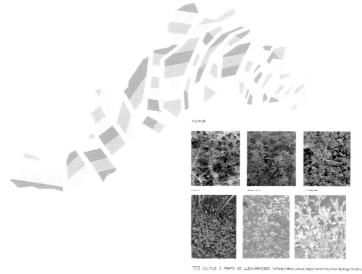

CULTIUS

▬▬ CULTIUS O PRATS DE LLEGUMINOSES (alfals,trèbol,lotus,veça,coronilla,anonis,Argyrolobium,doryonium)

- Four components of the vegetation strategy. Line of trees, lower and taller bushes on the slopes, agricultural crops on the terraces.
- Aerial view of the new landfill landscape in the Garraf area near Barcelona.
- Detail with symbolic significance. Nature gradually recolonizes a completely artificial topography.

- Image of the entrance area below. Sculpturing with residue material.
- The phasing of the whole project. Over a period of approximately ten years working its way uphill.
- Typical cross section of the soil layering, the terraced slopes, plantation and vegetation.

any heavily polluted leachate from the landfill, treats it and returns it to the new vegetation cover. The methane released from the landfill is recovered and used as a fuel for the water treatment plant. The mounds of rubble added to stabilize the huge mass of waste gave the designers the idea of cutting terraces into the slopes. These were so steep that in places ten-metre high retaining walls had to be built and the intervening spaces filled with sand and stones, separated by an impervious layer. Where trees and bushes were planted, the fertility of the topsoil was improved by adding fertiliser; organic compost and green manures (Leguminosae) were used on the terraces.

The design employs three types of planting: rows of pine trees flank the drainage canal and the paths; bushes have been planted on the slopes between the terraces; and the terraces have been sown with alternating green manures and agricultural species. The careful mix of intensively and extensively managed vegetation should eventually create a complete valley ecosystem with various stages of vegetation succession. The maintenance of the terraces is being monitored and supervised for the first two years by the architects. Local farmers perform the day-to-day work, noting which species become successfully established and which prove vulnerable, and removing unwanted invasive species.

The jury praised the intelligent open-ended strategy for breathing new life into the Vall d'en Joan. In contrast with many other landfills in Europe, it has been transformed into an attractive, sculptured landscape open to the public.

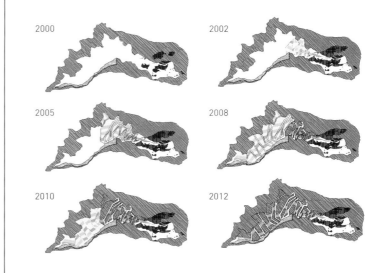

2000 2002 2005 2008 2010 2012

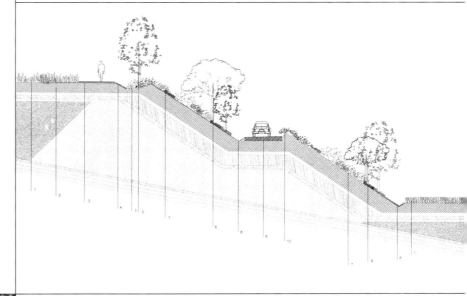

173

Jardin Portuaire

Programme A temporary garden over the course of four days on an abandoned quay in the port of Le Havre
Designer Thilo Folkerts Landschaftsarchitektur
Client Association Jardins Temporaires
Area 100 m^2
Design period 2000-2001
Implementation period 2001
Cost € 500

| ◃ To bring the water of the deep basins closer to the people, the landscape architect placed 80 plastic bags on a quay and filled them with water from the harbour. (Photo: Arnauld Duboys Fresney)

A harbour garden, a garden in the harbour – that sounds paradoxical. This should be where containers are shipped and cargos discharged, where machinery roars and men pour sweat... However, the part of the harbour where this garden was created is undergoing transition. No longer suitable for modern container technology, it has not yet been won over by the nearby city centre for residential, office and commercial buildings. This was the venue of the four-day "Les Jardins Temporaires" event held for the second time in July 2001, where some twenty landscape architects set up installations that were not so much to serve as prototypes for conventional open space designs in public or private

The Le Havre people discovered the disused harbour area in a way they had never seen it before and may get ideas for the spaces that will be built there in the future.
(Photo: Arnauld Duboys Fresney)

space but to create a world of visions. The harbour's transitional state allowed projects between imagination and reality, between experiment and duration, between learning to see and seeing. The people of Le Havre at least saw their harbour the way they had never seen it before. They discovered it as a garden with qualities that they may now ask for of those building the city to arise here in future.

One of these qualities is water. Thilo Folkerts' installation dealt with this water. Paradoxically, while water distinguishes a harbour it is inaccessible to people. Its depth can be gauged from looking at the basin; its expanse surmised by the horizon. To bring it up closer, Folkerts chose an area of about 100 square metres on a quay and placed 80 rectangular transparent plastic bags, heat-sealed all around, in an orthogonal grid. He filled the bags through an inconspicuous hole at the top with water from the harbour basin. The bags thus bulged out into pillows resembling jellyfish lying on the asphalt. Like windows, they provided views of the harbour water inside them, including all the flotsam: rubbish, aquatic plants, algae, little crabs. Hardly anyone would ever have experienced the water of a harbour basin right in front of his nose in this way. Each pillow thus invited people to carefully observe its contents, which obviously turned out to be more than water.

Contemplation was accompanied by action. Folkerts himself filled up the water pillows during all four days with a watering can, a hose and a small pump. With one pillow holding about 100 litres, the job was an exercise in patience. Once filled with water, the soft, shiny, wobbly and warm pillows virtually asked visitors to touch, sit and jump on them. Because the little fill holes remained open, the pillows could not burst and the water could squirt out in jets when children jumped around on them – fun for visitors but more work for the designer, who had to keep refilling. He looked after his project like a gardener, and the pillows grew, withered and grew back again, displaying themselves in different colours under the changing light of the sky.

The jury's discussion on this project was controversial. Some opined that it is not a garden but a performance. Exactly, this is radical and therefore outstanding, was the counterclaim. Others felt strongly attracted by the space, the pillows and the water in the pillows but then repelled because they thought the water was polluted. The fact that it was suited for play after all and revealed all of its gentleness eventually convinced the jurors, as did the contradictory feelings that this garden evoked.

Cardada geological observatory and trails

Programme A series of
landscape interventions
on a mountain
Designer Paolo L. Bürgi
Client Cardada Impianti
Turistici SA, Orselina-Locarno
Area not applicable
Design period 1995-2000
Implementation period
2000-2001
Cost € 1,544,000

The mountain of Cardada stands above Lake Maggiore in the southern Swiss Alps. Here Paolo Bürgi has made a story of journey and of prospect. Cardada is on the Insubrian line, the division between the European and African tectonic plates, a part a 90-million-year-old geological process. There is also a remarkable panorama, offering views of the Monte Rosa massif, the highest point of Switzerland, extending as far as the Italian Dolomites, as well as to the Maggia Delta between Locarno and Ascona – the lowest point of Switzerland.

You arrive via a modern cable-car system onto Bürgi's entrance platform, the Place for Encounters. This is a *Val Maggia* gneiss-covered square with a rigorous design, arranged so that the grass joints between the paving widen towards the edge of the cliff. A fountain, carved out of a tree trunk, counters the strict simplicity of the paving. From here, new connecting trails have been arranged so as to provide views of particular, large, specimen trees. Hiking thus becomes a way of learning to see something that was always there with different eyes. A trail leads to the Promontorio paesaggistico, a suspended passageway made of steel and titanium that rises up through the trees to a lookout platform, with an unexpected view of Lake Maggiore, the Brissago Islands, and beyond to a spectacular horizon of mountains.

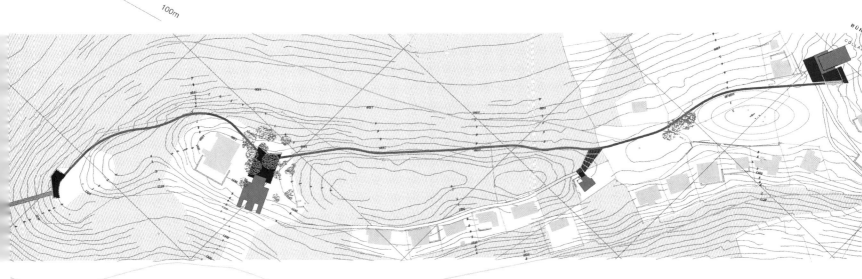

100m

Groundplan showing the path.
The views from the summit of Cardada extend along Lake Maggiore to beyond the Italian border to the south and to the Italian Dolomites. (Photo: Giosanna Crivelli)
The Promontorio paesaggistico rises up through the trees.
A fountain carved from a tree trunk counters the simple gneiss stone paving.

179

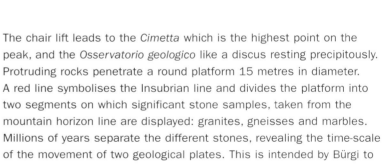

The chair lift leads to the *Cimetta* which is the highest point on the peak, and the *Osservatorio geologico* like a discus resting precipitously. Protruding rocks penetrate a round platform 15 metres in diameter. A red line symbolises the Insubrian line and divides the platform into two segments on which significant stone samples, taken from the mountain horizon line are displayed: granites, gneisses and marbles. Millions of years separate the different stones, revealing the time-scale of the movement of two geological plates. This is intended by Bürgi to promote awareness, experience and reflection.

The descent from Cardada allows a walk in the woods, going around the mountain from east to west on a "ludic path" which has been designed as an opportunity to reveal significant trees and for walkers to amuse themselves with unusual "games" scattered along the trail.

± Forest trails are part of the way one explores this mountain. (Photo: Cesare Micheletti)
▲ Simplicity of detailing everywhere.
▸▲ The Promontorio Paesaggistico, a suspension bridge-like lookout of steel and titanium rises through the trees. (Photo: Giosanna Crivelli)

‡ Plan of the Cimetta.
▲ The circular Cimetta is lined with geological samples from the mountains beyond and elegantly and minimally fenced.
‹ Cimetta aerial view with the line representing the Insubrian line.

181

Playgrounds for Daubeney primary school

Programme Playgrounds for
a primary school in London's
East End
Designers Kinnear Landscape
Architects
In collaboration with Hattie
Coppard, Snug and Outdoor
Client Hackney Wick Public
Art Programme
Area 900 m²
Design period 2000-2002
Implementation period
2002-2003
Cost € 120,000

- ◂ ▴ Colour and light.
- ◂ Po.yurethane-based industrial paint transforms this macadam yard.
- ▴ The project is about pattern and colour changing spaces. The project was an experiment to add playfulness in public spaces without actually providing lots of formal play equipment and using instead "light, colour, movement and time".
- ◂ ▾ The slot.
- ▾ Grcund plan.

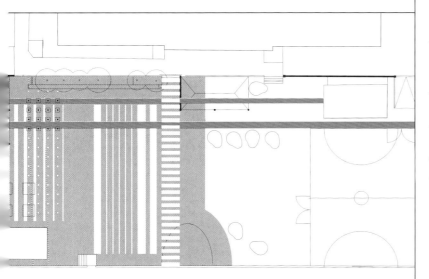

In Britain many urban schools have a macadam schoolyard dominated by a Victorian School Board building and surrounded by high walls. It is a challenge to make these places richer, pleasanter and more stimulating. Daubeney primary school in London's East End is a typical Victorian school with 485 pupils, from three to eleven years, from a large number of ethnic and cultural backgrounds. There are two playgrounds, one for infants and a larger one for juniors. The site has narrow garden areas with mature trees on one side, two shelters and a little seating. Football dominated all the activities and it was frenetic, noisy and, sometimes, violent. There was an absence of shade and a shortage of seats.

The Daubeney Experimental Playground Project began in 1999 inspired by a series of seminars entitled Artists in School Grounds. This led to the Hackney Wick Public Art Programme and a week's programme of workshops for the schoolchildren organized by artist Hattie Coppard in March 2000. It was recognized that children and adults generally find it difficult to express their feelings about space, and to imagine and articulate possible changes. The project aimed to draw out conscious and subconscious thoughts, fears and desires about the playground, and to enable participants to imagine new ways of using and seeing familiar spaces. The week's consultation also required the children to co-operate with each other to make the project.

The designers, trying to make a playful space which is not a playing area, were particularly interested in the function of the whole space and the relationships between different territories. They capitalized on the essential openness of the traditional school playground and – without use

- Cone circle: part of an early workshop before the playground was redesigned.
- No physical barriers.
- Moving islands: 45 centimetre high, large galvanised steel planters, in which the children grow flowers from seed and which create places to chat and play.

of physical barriers – to find ways of defining distinct spaces or zones within it. They also used high-quality and durable materials, in preference to cheap-and-cheerful solutions, which do not last.

The issue of football dominating the playground had already been identified as a problem and an early decision had been taken by the school, independently of the project, to screen off an area for ball games. Linking the junior and younger playground was also important so that the big playground was not so hidden, secret and scary. Making a place in the playground where one can be higher than every one else is exciting and leads to creative play focused around this element. Using reflective surfaces that bring light into dark spaces changes the role of the existing shelter from being dark, damp, and unwelcoming to a place where children genuinely want to spend time and that will encourage co-operative play.

The spaces were then boldly transformed using polyurethene paint, steel planters to involve the children with plant growth, rotating platforms and poles and screens of cloth. In May 2003 the school hosted a week-long residency for a poet and a dancer. Performances from these workshops were used as the opening ceremony for the playground. The poetry and dancing workshops were briefed to interpret the playground in their own ways. The poet Kit Wright ran the poetry workshops and these worked particularly well. The poems produced by the children described imagined environments stimulated by the patterns and shapes of the playground.

The goddess speaks

Once I click my fingers,
There's our beautifull playground,
White, yellow and pink stripes.

I stamp my feet
And there's our hill,
With a mirror to see our reflection.

This is the best playground,
Bright and colourfull.
I made it look so tempting.
It could be the best playground ever
Made by me... the goddess.

This playground isn't here
For a few years,
With my power,
It's here forever.

I'm the goddess of this wondelfull playground.

Montana

The poles

The poles remind me of big trees in the forest,
A spaceship in an alien landscape,
Tall sunflowers
That peep over large garden walls.
Listen carefully, you can hear,
Yellow snakes are hissing!

Leah

≛ The use of mirrors adds a window and expands the schoolyard beyond the boundaries
of the Victorian yard.
– The forest of poles.
➤ The playground has been filled with play.

Fünf Höfe courtyards and rooftops

Programme Design of inner
courts and rooftops in
connection with conversion
and new construction in a
historic perimeter block of
buildings to create an ensemble
for retail and gastronomic
establishments, offices, an art
gallery and passageways open
to the public
Designer Burger
Landschaftsarchitekten
in collaboration with
Herzog & de Meuron
(architecture, creative direction),
Hilmer & Sattler (architecture),
Tita Giese, Bernhard Häring
(hanging gardens)
Client HypoVereinsbank
Immobilien AG, Munich
Owner Deutsche Immobilien
Fonds AG, Hamburg
Area 4,438 m^2
Design period 1998-2001
Implementation period
2001-2003

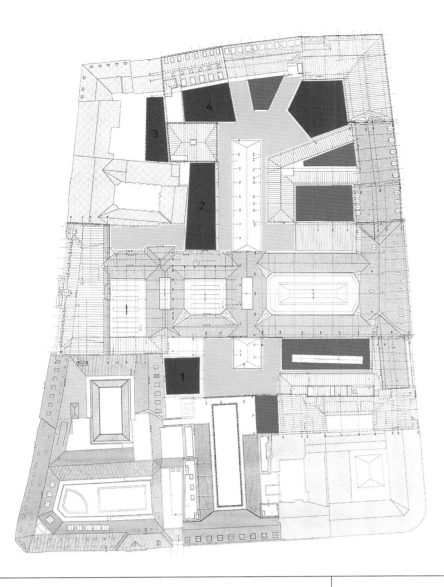

The art gallery of the HypoVereinsbank was for a long time the only public place in the massive building complex belonging to the bank on Theatiner Street in the historic centre of Munich. The old buildings faced passers-by as an impenetrable block, with only the shop windows of stores on the ground floor enlivening the façade. With a competition in the early 90s, the bank rang in the changes for the site – the brief called for a concept for a transparent combination of art, retail and gastronomy, with passageways cutting through it. Its name was to be "Fünf Höfe" (Five Courtyards). The architects Herzog & de Meuron of Basel won the competition, but with a design that was too close to a "clear-cutting" kind of urban renewal and therefore impossible to get accepted politically in Munich. The bank finally gave the commission to two architecture firms, Herzog & de Meuron and Hilmer & Sattler of Munich, with the stipulation that they start all over again. The client and the architects in charge took on the Munich landscape architect Susanne Burger in 1998 and asked her to provide a design concept for the open spaces.

This time the architects dealt more carefully with the existing fabric, preserving over 50 percent of it. Only a narrow strip of the façade along Theatiner Street betrays the contemporary architecture with its curtain of perforated sheet copper that Munich residents promptly nicknamed "the coat of mail". The architects laid out a sequence of passageways through the historic urban lot and thus created not only new shopping areas but also ingenious indoor realms and new routes through the previously impenetrable block. They also referred to the surrounding green spaces in the old town by installing a hanging garden by Tita Giese in the central Salvator Passageway. Here a garden of potted climbers, placed on a

The architects created a sequence of passageways leading through the historic urban lot transformed into shopping areas. The landscape architects counterbalanced these places of teeming activity with a series of four quiet courtyards. Represented in yellow are the landscaped rooftops.
1 Portia courtyard
2 Promenade courtyard
3 Garden courtyard
4 Amira courtyard
◄ | ▾ Views from the Pranner passageway to the Portia courtyard. Visitors pass through a curtain of water that extends the perforation motif of the facade.
(Photos: Margherita Spiluttini)

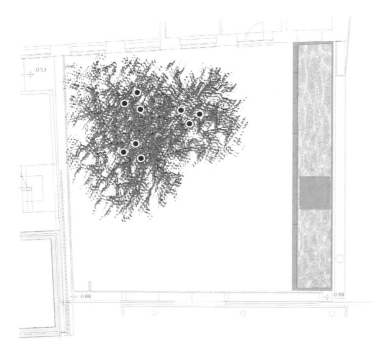

‹ Ground plan of Portia courtyard.

˅ Portia courtyard is a simple square of pebbles from the river Isar and only features three Kobushi magnolia trees to form a contrast with the straight lines of the buildings. (Photo: Boris Storz (bottom))

grating at ceiling level, creates the impression of a green baldachin. Underneath, you can "shop 'til you drop", as in all the other passageways.

The landscape architects missed a quiet counterpart to the places teeming with activity. They therefore complemented the continual series of passageways with a connected series of courtyards remote from the hustle and bustle. In contrast to the continuous design of the passageways, they gave each court a special character of its own. Each responds in a different way to the architecture. The jury noted with admiration that here one could not tell where the architecture ends and the landscape begins and that the tiny open spaces develop extraordinary spatial power next to the architecture.

Off the Pranner Passageway, the Portia Courtyard proclaims itself as a simple square of pebbles from the River Isar and serves as a tranquil terrace for the adjacent café. A curtain of water forms a filter towards the lively passageway, its drops extending the perforated motif of "the coat of mail" down to the ground. A little pool also separates the passageway from the court: visitors cross a square stepping-stone to get in. Only the three magnolia trees (*Magnolia denudata*) break up the straight lines and mineral materials of the Portia courtyard with the bizarre way they grow. The Promenade Courtyard responds to the greenery growing down from

◄ | ▲ The maple varieties of the Promenade courtyard perform a colourful play visible from the glazed shops. (Photo: Florian Holzherr)

▼ Ground plan of Promenade courtyard.

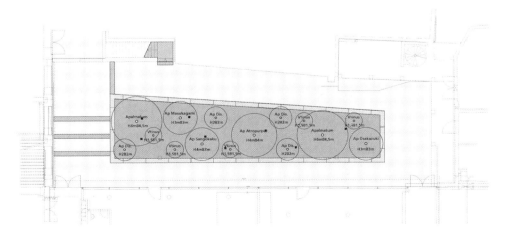

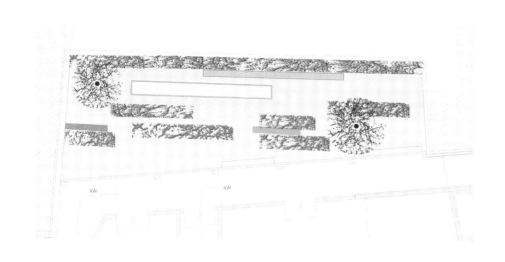

◂ ▴ Ground plan of Garden courtyard.
◂ The towel-sized Garden courtyard opens up to the sky and is
conceived as a hedge theatre out of scene-shifting boxwood.
(Photos: Florian Holzherr (above) and Boris Storz)

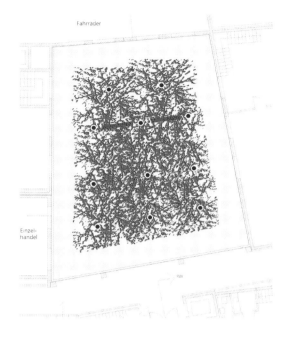

he ceiling in the Salvator Passageway with a backdrop of Japanese
rnamental maples arising from an elongated bed. Passers-by look
om the passageway through the fully glazed shops toward Promenade
ourtyard and see it as the background to a picture: a wood with an
ndulating ground level like green waves and tree masses shaped like
louds. The maple varieties (*Acer palmatum* in various varieties) were
elected to perform a colourful play, ranging from dark green through dark
ed to yellow-orange in autumn. The broad concrete edge enclosing the
ee bed is a good place to sit, a gravel path leads visitors around it, and
oncrete steps negotiate the slightly varying levels. Farther back is the
arden Courtyard, a towel-sized garden for the neighbouring flats. In order
o give it a feeling of space, the planners conceived it as a hedge theatre,
cene-shifting boxwood clipped into potato-like shapes, with yellow flowers
rst tickling its feet in spring until yellow-blooming perennials emerge
om behind in summer. It is fully open to the sky. The Amira Courtyard
elcomes visitors in completely the opposite way. In this square off a
econdary passageway, there are no windows on the ground floor opening
nto the courtyard and the sky is no more than a distant rectangle. Here
le landscape architects created a room by inserting a green ceiling
bove it and shutting out the shaft. Rising from the dark granite spread
n the ground, the heliophobic ironwood trees (*Parrotia persica*), which
an be shaped into canopies like plane trees, have a captivating rusty
utumn tint. Rounded concrete stones invite visitors to take a seat.
he majolica figure of a historical Munich "pigeon woman" wears a frost-
sistant wickerwork wrapping in winter. While visitors on the ground floor
xperience the Amira Courtyard as a room between the grey floor and the
een ceiling platform, people on the office storeys above see it as a soft
een pillow of foliage between the pale exterior walls.

◄ ▲ Ground plan of Amira courtyard.
▲ A canopy out of heliophobic ironwood trees creates a room in the formerly unattractive
  shaft of the Amira courtyard. (Photo: Boris Storz)
▼ The circular concrete tiles on the rooftops repeat the perforation motif of the facade.

Isar Plan inner-city river banks

Programme Design of the
riverbank to improve the
flood control measures,
fixed minimum runoff,
hydrodynamics, water quality,
recreation, conservation and
cityscape
Designer Irene Burkhardt
Landschaftsarchitekten
In collaboration with
Mahl-Gebhard Landschafts-
architekten, Reichenbach-
Klinke Schranner Architekten,
SKI GmbH + Co. KG Engineers

Client Munich Water
Department, City of Munich
Area 2 kilometres of riverbanks
of varying width along river Isar
Design period 2002
Implementation period
2005–2008
Cost € 7,500,000

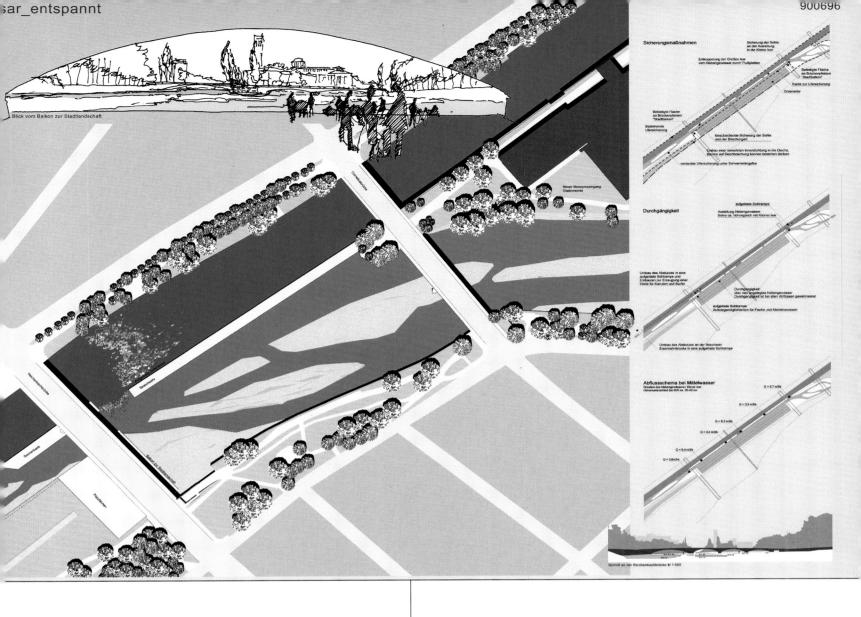

Munich is not far from the Alps. During snowmelt in spring, the waters
flood down the River Isar to the plains in raging torrents, passing the
city center. Understandably in the 19th century, hydraulic engineers
wanted to tame this wild alpine river. Within Munich the Isar was forced
into a channel. Since the 1950s a reservoir lake further up river in the
foothills of the Alps has regulated flows additionally. The Isar within the
city could no longer be perceived as a wild river.
Munich's residents nevertheless utilized the river and its environs as
they were: sunbathing on its gravel banks (where they remained), ball
games on the extensive, newly created alluvial meadows and promenades
along the tree-covered banks near the Deutsches Museum.

Channeling the river also caused problems: inadequate flood control and
poor water quality caused concern among the citzens of Munich. Views
and access to the river itself as well as the quality of the surrounding
open spaces were perceived as substandard.
In the 1980s redesigns were first discussed, but it took until 1995 for
the public authorities to commission a panel of experts to create a new
vision for the river – the "Isarplan". In 2000, the first measures were
put into practice. In the southernmost stretch of the river the concrete
channel walls were removed. The Isar was freed up to meander, islands,
gravel banks and beaches were formed. The resulting informal landscape
alongside the river is strongly reminiscent of the English Garden
(Munich's biggest and most beloved park). It matches everybody's
imagination of a more natural landscape and is much appreciated by
Munich's residents today.

▲ At the most central part of the riverbank, the design features a series of "river platforms"
that extend under the historic bridges and provide views "from the river" into town,
dividing off a branch from the river Isar, with islands and tranquil waters for play.
◄│▼ A hydraulically important weir is to be maintained in front of the Deutsches Museum;
the design takes over its straightness. The photos show the existing situation before
implementation of the design.
(Photos: David Emmer(lauter))

193

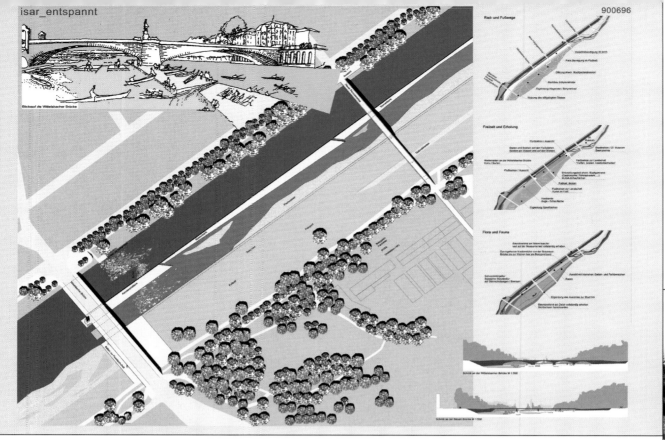

- On the river Isar's east bank between the bridges, the landscape architects use the alluvial meadows as an area for sports and games and transform the linear "river platforms" gradually into the more organically shaped landscape of the south.
- Playing children on the existing riverbanks before transformation.

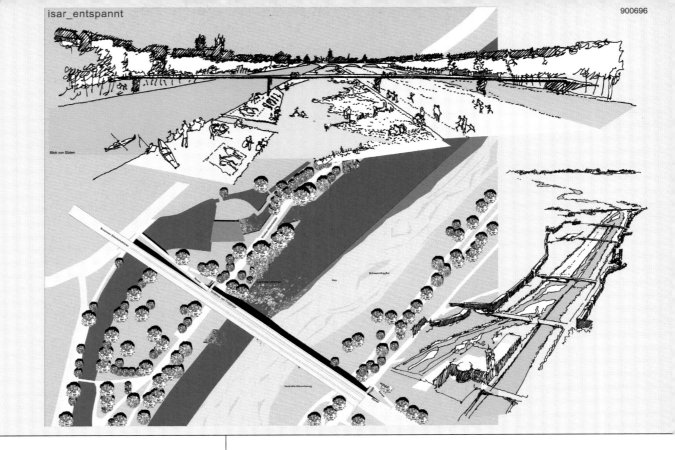

isar_entspannt

> In the south, the meandering forms of the river Isar are maintained by the landscape architects and offer opportunity for sunbathing and swimming while reinforcing the dams for flood protection.

- The photo shows the existing situation.

According to the authorities' wishes, the design of the inner-city part of the river was to break up this monochrome picture. In order to collect ideas, the public authorities held a competition among seven teams of landscape architects, urban planners and hydraulic engineers in 2002. As expected, the designs presented varying scenarios for the inner-city Isar, ranging from the familiar, almost natural, informal landscape picture to the linear urban one. The competition jury awarded the first prize to the team around the landscape architect Irene Burkhardt of Munich, thus – surprisingly – favouring an urban design. Burkhardt and her colleagues at first continue the organic shapes of the southern Isar landscape, but closer to the city centre they align them into a straight riverbank. On the east bank, they set up alluvial meadows where games and sports can still be played. Offshore, a row of platforms in the river continues all the way to the hydraulically important weir at the Deutsches Museum. These "river platforms" divide a branch from the Isar, here a racing stream. Boats can dock at them and behind them a recreational landscape extends with tranquil waters suitable for small children to play. The platforms lead under the Isar's historic bridges, forming balconies here and there and providing beautiful views "from the river" into town and from the bridges toward the banks. Where Museum Island noses between the main river and its branch (Große and Kleine Isar), small inaccessible islands shelter protected biotopes. The jury of the present publication particularly commended the design's simple and severe formal language, which creates a landscape picture that is urban. People animate it in summer, making the river into part of the city. On the other hand, the jury also felt that this picture is compelling in winter without people. The banks and the elements built into them seem like part of the river.

In Munich, however, this landscape picture could not find acceptance for political reasons. Citizens mobilized themselves and backed the second-prize-winning design of the team around Winfrid Jerney, which extends the natural-looking landscape of the south into the city centre. The compromise that is to be built jointly by both prize-winners now has of course lost the linearity of the winning design.

Location Munich (D)

Landschaftspark Riem

Programme Public park on the former site of Munich's airport
Designer Latitude Nord
In collaboration with
Stahr & Haberland (first phase), Luz Landschafts-architekten (second phase)
Client City of Munich, represented by MRG Maßnahmeträger Munich-Riem GmbH
Area 210 ha
Design period 1995

Implementation period
1997-2005
Cost € 37,000,000

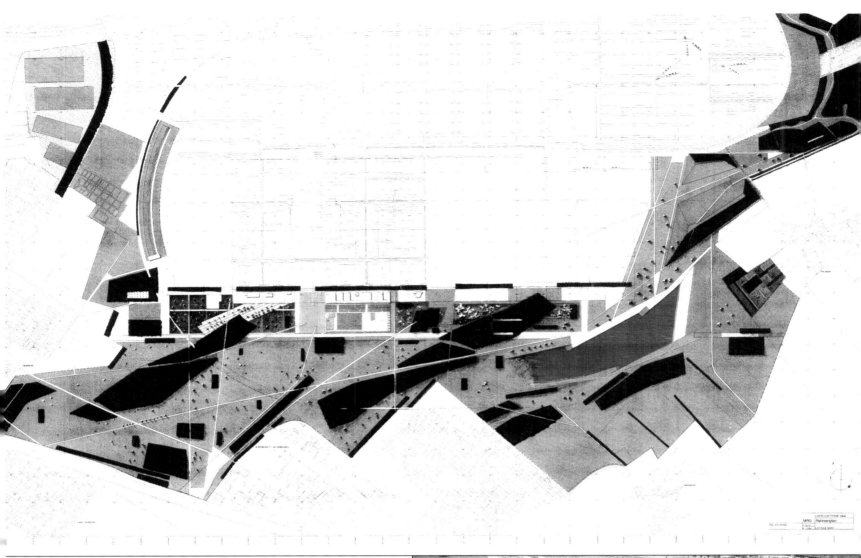

The former Riem Airport is an urban fringe site to the east of Munich. The old airfield, which was Munich's main postwar airport, closed in 1992. Part of the site is being developed as an urban extension around the new Munich trade fair *Messestadt*, with dwellings for 16 000 residents and employment for 13 000 people. Planning dedicated one third of the area to housing, one third to trade fair and one third to green spaces and the total development will take fifteen years. So the idea is to first build a large public park which will increase the appeal of the area from the outset. The park, the trade fair and the first part of the new town were scheduled to be finished in 2005, the year in which Munich hosted the major federal garden festival (or Bundesgartenschau, BUGA 05). The city has aimed to use BUGA 05 to present the new Riem development and its park to the public. The BUGA show gardens were installed predominantly on future development plots to the west. They were removed after the show and left a permanent piece of landscape architecture, a city park, just as Munich's Westpark was a previous International Garden Festival (an IGA) in 1983 and the Olympiapark was a major new park, in the north of the city, in 1972.

The site is on the flat, open plain east of Munich and is a classic urban fringe site. To the north-east is the new *Messestadt* development of business parks, housing, shops and exhibition halls. To the south-east lies farmland and woodland with views across the plain to the Alps. The design competition for the Riem Park took place in 1995 and was won by the French team of Latitude Nord headed by Gilles Vexlard and Laurence Vacherot. Their design combined the open meadows with the woodlands by planting two large woodland blocks on an open field, accentuating

◂ Two large woodland blocks are planted on the open field, accentuated with smaller groves, hedges and individual trees along the diagonal walkways that are reminiscent of the historical field pattern. (Photo: MRG)
◸ Design drawing for the Riem Park.
◂ Planes sculptured by volumes of vegetation. (Photo: BUGA)

them with smaller groves, hedges or individual trees placed along diagonal walkways that were reminiscent of the historical field pattern (and partly follow the footprints of the old runways). The spaces of this park are in a state of free flow; there are no boundaries with the surrounding urban settlements and the cultural landscape to the east. Space is created in a very subtle manner by slightly inclining the terrace to the south, and the meadows to the north, as if landscape architecture was a play of tectonic plates that are sculpted by volumes of vegetation.

A "band of activities" crosses the site east-west and is bounded on the south by a two-kilometre long, 180-metre wide raised terrace. This terrace marks the edge of the urban border of east-west orthogonal plots and the open park landscape to the south. To the north some of the show gardens will be permanent and will be active recreation facilities. To the south are meadows on the poorer soils allowing passive recreational uses. To the east the "band of activities" leads to water margin planting around a large new swimming lake and to two *Rodelhügel* (great mounds) for snow sledging.

In the southern meadows, Latitude Nord has designed a bold, large-scale and formal arrangement of spaces created by trees arranged in woodland blocks, in groves of row trees and also by hedges. The blocks are of oak (*Quercus*) or of pine (*Pinus sp.*). The monospecific groves are of row trees whether used as larger structural elements aligned east-west consisting of small leaved lime (*Tilia cordata*) or scattered lines of common ash (*Fraxinus excelsior*). The lines of the trees reflect and follow farmland and urban plot lines and are also determined by the prevailing winds. The

▸ The structure of the park is deducted from the analysis of the region and its woodland composition, its hydrology, and its historic field pattern.
▾ Spaces in between the woodland blocks have scattered individual specimen trees. (Photo: Horst Burger)

▾ | ▸ ▾ The swimming lake features a hard edge to the north, with an urban promenade and flights of steps linking the new town to the water. (Photo: Horst Burger)

◂ ⚡ Concrete elements such as walkways and low walls underline the formal arrangement.

◂ ⚡ A two-kilometre long, 180-metre wide terrace crosses Landschaftspark Riem east-west, formed by parallel strips of pavement, gravel paths and strips of lawn. From here, different perspectives open or close the view. To the east two mounds for snow sledging indicate the eastern end of the park; to the south an artificial swimming lake evolved into a sunbathers' paradise.

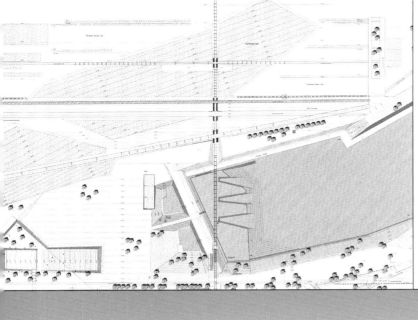

spaces in between have scattered individual specimen trees. To the
north, dark colours draw a hard edge in front of the buildings, to the
south, light colours merge with the sunlight and blur the limits of the
park.

The large ten-hectare swimming lake is fed by groundwater. The water
level varies, the natural groundwater table was between seven and eight
metres below the surface and had to be raised and stabilized to a depth
of three metres below the surface by a complex engineering process;
as a result the lake is now visible from afar. A 150 metre-long beach can
accomodate 10,000 visitors, and is bordered by lawns and has evolved
into a sunbathers' paradise. The two great mounds for snow sledging are
made of 700,000 cubic metres of fill from the site.

German Garden Festivals designs are challenging: they have to provide
for the temporary installation of a range of small, contained show garden
spaces and for large numbers of people in the first year while also
providing a major new public park. At Riem the masterplan corrals the
temporary show gardens in an enclosed area to the north, within an
orthogonal formality. Latitude Nord has arranged this enclosed formal
area within a much larger landscape framework, which again recalls in
part the wide open spaces of the airport. The new park celebrates, with
an almost brutal frankness, open parkland effects composed by the
formal carving out of spaces from regular tree planting in rows and
blocks. In the view of the jury of the present book this is "a park at the
scale of Munich, very legible, very formal… the work of a European
Master and it deserves respect."

↑ Detail of the western border of the swimming lake.
◄ Detail of one of the mounds.
▼ Bronze elements are incorporated in the wall accompanying the two-kilometre long
terrace, showing aerial views of selected landscapes situated on the same degree of
latitude.

Odda Torg marketplace and waterfront

Programme Transformation of a working quay into open urban space
Designer Svein Erik Bergem (design), Lail Iren Isene, Rune Vik, Jostein Bjørbekk (project manager), Bjørbekk & Lindheim AS
In collaboration with Ketil Kiran, Archus AS and Braathen & Thorvaldsen AS
Client City of Odda
Area 4,300 m^2
Design period 1999-2002
Implementation period 2002-2003
Cost € 1,040,000

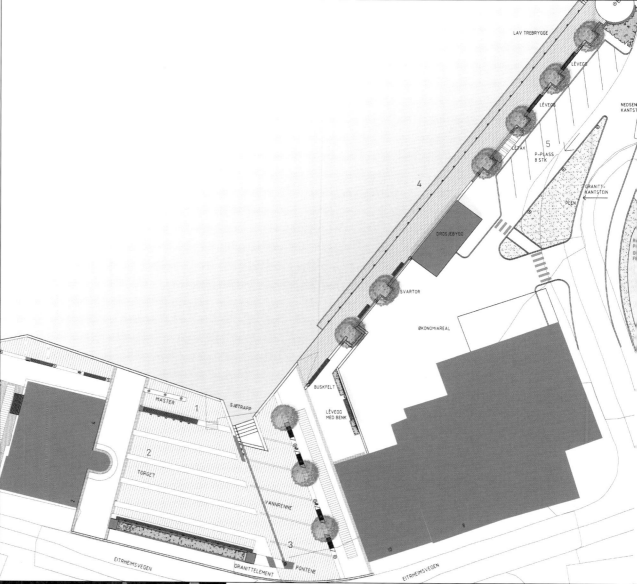

Plan.
1 Masts
2 Market plan
3 Fountain
4 Boardwalk
5 Car park
Formerly the quayside was dominated by parked cars. (Photo: Jostein Bjørbekk)

Odda is not a pretty town by Norwegian standards, it is a small industrial town of some 7,500 inhabitants best known for its astonishing nature and for the plant with zinc production. It is located at the head of the Hardanger Fjord, which is an extremely long fjord, south-east of Bergen. The views northward from the town, up the fjord, which is embraced by the Hardangervidda mountains, are sublime. In spring there is the blossom of fruit trees along the shore, with views of the ice of the Folgefanna Glacier above. This position and its views have been exploited by Bjørbekk and Lindheim's design for a waterfront market place.

The town council wished to rejuvenate the centre, which has always been the quayside, provide a market and link the east and west sides of town via, what had been, a working quay which then fell into disuse and became a car park. The project started with a sketch by architect Ketil Kiran. Then Bjørbekk & Lindheim was invited to do the design and construction descriptions. The landscape architects have emphasized the market place's hard landscape character by focussing on finely detailed grey granite stonework. Planting is limited to a beech (Fagus sylvatica) hedge and row of alder trees (Alnus glutinosa), which provide a wind break.

The main square is at a corner of the waterside, between two existing waterside buildings. The square is paved with grey granite, marked by stripes of lighter granite and crossed by a water runnel which is fed by a fountain. The runnel leads down some steps into the fjord. Three mast like poles complete the scene. The eastern section has an oak boardwalk along the water's edge, lined by benches protected by timber walls also in

203

▲ The boardwalk along the quay, designed by Rune Vik, is a suntrap, sheltered by timber screens. (Photo: Dan-Erik Aggvin)

▸ The new quayside market-place, formerly a car park. (Photo: Laila Iren Isene)

oak, so you can sit facing the setting sun. The jury's verdict was that the design is "not overdone, controlled, well detailed, not too much, not too little. The right things in the right place". This is a classic scheme of urban renewal, landscape design acting as a catalyst and providing a focus of identity and community for a town, which has had economic problems.

Finely detailed grey granite stonework. (Photo: Laila Iren Isene)
▴ The views northward up the Hardanger fjord, embraced by the Hardangervidda mountains are sublime.
A fountain feeds a rill which crosses the marketplace.

Le jardin sauvage

Programme New museum garden serving as art in public space in the areaway between avenue de Président Wilson and Palais de Tokyo (Contemporary Arts Centre)
Designer Marck Pouzol, Laurent Dugua, Véronique Faucheur, atelier le balto
In collaboration with Pré Carré
Client French Ministry of Culture and Communication, Fine Arts Division
Area 800 m^2
Design period 2001
Implementation period 2002
Cost € 100,000

▸   The gap between the unstuccced foundations of Palais de Tokyo and the masonry arches of the Metro tunnel once was a rubbish tip and has evolved into a wild piece of landscape.
(Photos: Yann Monel)

wo weeks was all the time the landscape architects had for realizing this
arden. As a commission for art in public space at the Palais de Tokyo in
'aris, for which the directors of the Contemporary Arts Centre contracted
he Berlin firm of Le Balto, the derelict unsightly areaway between the
treet and the building was to be cleared out and filled with new life by
he time the Centre opened.

he Palais de Tokyo, up to now the home of the Museum of Modern Art,
s a monumental building dating from the 1930s set up on the slope of
he right bank of the Seine. Making clever use of the topography, the
uilding opens toward the valley with a terrace and provides views across
he Seine and the historic skyline of the Rive Gauche. The Eiffel Tower is
ght opposite. No wonder that the entrance at the back of Palais de
okyo, where the building towers high along the avenue du Président
Vilson, led a shadowy existence. Between the pavement and the façade
'as a gaping areaway, walled in between the unstuccoed foundations
f the building and the masonry arches of the Métro tunnel under the
venue. It was the kind of place that offers itself as a rubbish tip
'hich is what it looked like until the museum was rededicated as the
ontemporary Arts Centre and the Bordelaise architects Anne Lacaton
nd Jean-Philippe Vassal gave it a new interior architecture.
reed of rubbish, it presented itself to the landscape architects as a
raughty place without sunlight, facing the ventilation outlets of the
alais de Tokyo and enclosed by 20 to 40-metre-high walls that felt rather
verwhelming. Only extreme unobtrusiveness and full physical involvement
ould transform this place into something like an enchanted garden – it
till sends shivers down the visitor's spine, but the feeling of curiosity and
ascination with the unknown predominates.

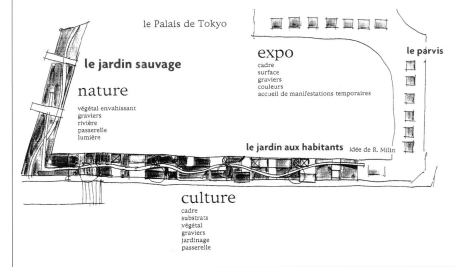

le Palais de Tokyo

le jardin sauvage

nature

végétal envahissant
graviers
rivière
passerelle
lumière

expo

cadre
surface
graviers
couleurs
accueil de manifestations temporaires

le parvis

le jardin aux habitants idée de R. Milin

culture

cadre
substrats
végétal
graviers
jardinage
passerelle

◂ | ▾ A boardwalk, 70 centimetres above the ground, lifts visitors towards the light and forms a discovery trail through the garden.

The landscape architects first extended a boardwalk, about 70 centimetres above the ground, along the areaway. This lifts visitors toward the light, lessens the oppressiveness of the walls and lays out a discovery trail through the garden. Vertical trellis cables along the walls draw clematis and other climbing plants upward, and cables braced from wall to wall frame sections of the sky. The landscape architects installed the sprinkler system at a height of six metres. Finally, with 150 different species of heliophobic plants they brought the life of the wilderness into the areaway. Climbing roses (*Rosa Kiftsgate*) have since taken over the masonry, hydrangeas (*Hortensia petiolaris*) are occupying the leftover concrete, trees of heaven (*Ailanthus altissima*) incline over the boardwalk, knotweed (*Polygonum sacchalinensis*) proliferates on piles of crushed stone, and perennials such as hostas, butterbur (*Petasites*) and others knot a dense carpet on the ground. A handmade iron-barred gate of the kind that belongs in such a wild garden closes off the new realm.

Not only the gate was made by hand. The short time at their disposal required the landscape architects to add specialists with the necessary handicraft skills to their team and even to use their own hands. The planners themselves built, planted, dug and watered here, they created space with the means they were able to handle themselves, with no more and no less. It was the planners' attitude that convinced the jury. The jurors clearly recognized the planners' intent to design without "design" and to make an inhospitable place into a lively garden, which inspires reflection upon where wilderness ends and creativity begins, where the artificial intervention is what allows the presence of the natural in the first place. By making a garden, the planners have retrieved this place for people, and the jury appreciates its very special atmosphere: "one big shadow, filled with plants".

Perennials such as hostas, butterbur and others knit a dense carpet on the ground.
A handmade iron-barred gate closes off the area and lends it the spirit of an enchanted garden.

Waldpark Potsdam

Programme Urban park on a former military training ground
Designer B+B stedebouw en landschapsarchitectuur
Client BUGA Potsdam
Area 16 ha
Design period 1998–1999
Implementation period 2001
Cost € 3,000,000

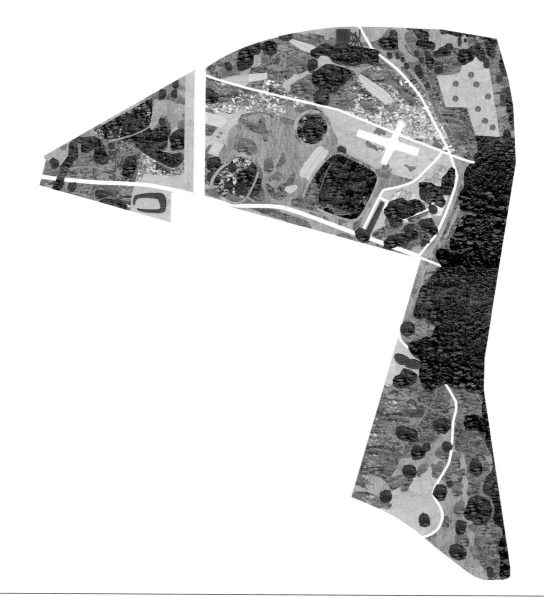

‣ Design drawing for the Waldpark.
▾ The design was based on zoning studies: valuable biotopes, biotopes of limited value, biotopes of no value, intensive-extensive use, plan.

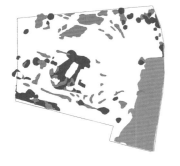

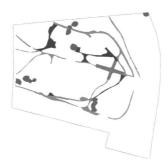
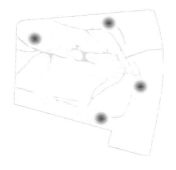
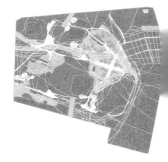

In 1998 the developer Bornstedter Feld in Potsdam, Germany, held a design competition for the Waldpark. This park lies in the Volkspark Bornstedter Feld, a former Russian training camp dating from the DDR era. The aim of the competition was to produce a plan for the park that retains the valuable elements while providing for intensive use. On the one hand, the old wooded landscape with the relics of its military past has to be preserved; on the other hand, the regenerated Waldpark has to provide room for sports and complement the historic Royal Gardens elsewhere in Potsdam. In 2001 the park was part of the Bundesgartenschau.

Dutch planning and landscape design consultants B+B of Amsterdam carried off the first prize. The jury finds this to be a watertight plan. Intensive uses are distributed around the edges of the park, while the emphasis in the central area is on conservation and improving valuable habitats. Various zoning models were used to map out the locations of the most valuable habitats, the less valuable ones, the areas of no special value and the best areas for intensive use. A composite map of all these layers formed the basis for the final design.

In some places falling trees are a hazard. Surrounded by walls of tree trunks and branches, these hidden areas are like safe havens dotted in the park, and have become interesting areas for biological research. A network of paths with loose surfacing and glass lead the visitor to the accessible areas and to the four meeting points on the edge of the park. The central grassy area can also be used as an in formal recreation area.

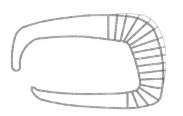

▲ Paths made from loose surfacing and glass.
▸ Jumping, hanging, lying, sitting: it's all possible.
▸ ▾ Sliding.
▾ Play equipment forms a clear landmark.

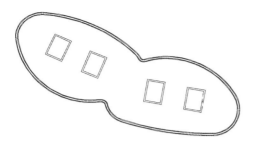

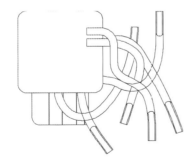

Each meeting point has its own special piece of play equipment. These are not pieces of standard playground equipment, but hard sculptures with organic shapes. They can be used to hang from, sit on or lie in, and for skating, sliding, climbing and jumping. Although each one invites different types of activity, the designers have introduced a certain element of uniformity. All four have an unusual architectural form inspired by the war-time bunkers dispersed throughout the site. They have been built of a reddish sprayed concrete to make them stand out against the green woods, turning the play sculptures into landmarks. But even though the structures have been lauded in many publications, one member of the selection committee could only see large "dirty" elements.

The selection committee judged the plan by B+B to be a wonderful example of how to transform an existing woodland into an urban park with just a few tactical interventions. As one of the members put it, the Waldpark is an exceptional cultural dialogue between old and new.

213

Terraces of the Nový Smíchov shopping centre

Programme Roof garden
on a shopping mall
Designer D3A spol. s.r.o.
In collaboration with Florart
(horticulture)
Client Carrefour & Delcis
Area 1.5 ha
Design period 1995-1999
Implementation period
2000-2002
Cost € 84,500

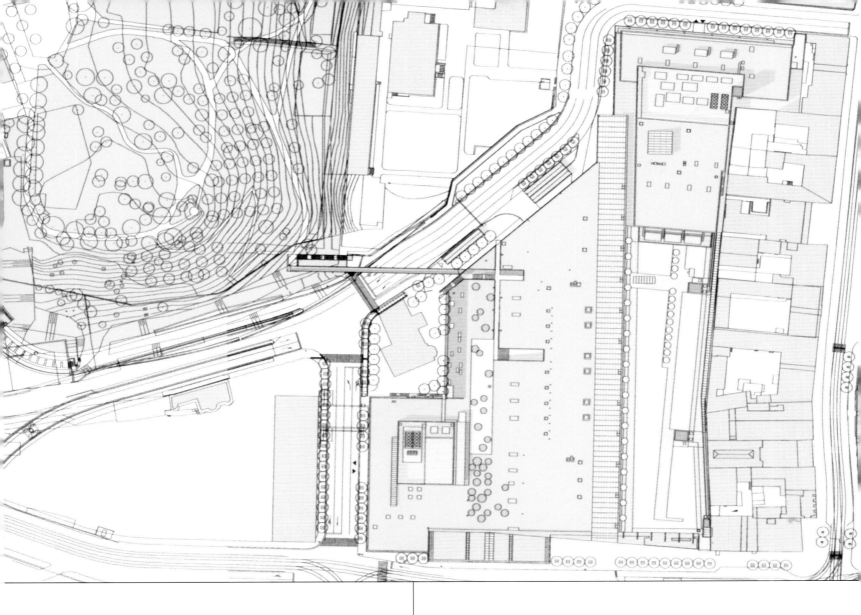

At the foot of the hill of Sacre Coeur and just west of Jiráskuv. Bridge in Smíchov is one of Prague's new shopping malls: Nový Smíchov, which consists of 60,000 square metres of retail development including a big Carrefour and Delcis department store, food courts, multiplex cinemas and a games arcade. The development is of interest because it is built on the grounds of an old factory overlooked by the hills above and, as part of the planning conditions, the architects were required to provide a "green" roof. This vegetated roof is extensive: 14,500 square metres in expanse and planted with grasses and herbs. It forms a series of inaccessible terraces that gently slope westwards from the glazed shopping mall and descend to a flat, publicly accessible area with concrete paving and a grass lawn. A distinctive part of the design is the remarkable 13-metre high grass wall, set at 58 degrees. This is even steeper than the well-known Omnisports grassed pyramid in Paris.

The steep slopes and the terraces are planted with a mix of drought tolerant grasses (*Festuca rubra, Festuca ovina* and *Poa pratensis*) and herbaceous plants (*Allium schoenoprasum, Sedum album, Sedum acre, Thymus pulegioides* and *Thymus serpyllum*). This herbaceous and grass mix is intended to reflect and give the same impression as the rough grass hills above. The flat lawn area is intensively irrigated and planted with *Festuca rubra, Festuca ovina* and *Poa pratensis* on 35 centimetres of topsoil. There is also a grove of plane trees (*Platanus acerifolia*) planted in tree pits of five cubic metres each, which are built into the roof space. The roof is reinforced concrete, but the tree pits descend though the concrete deck to a lower structure of steelwork, which forms a second deck structure which is used as a service area. The terraces and the

- Situation and urban ground plan.
- A prairie which is a roof garden planted with drought tolerant grasses.
- At the bottom of this view is the hill of Sacre Coeur with Nový Smíchov in the middle and beyond the River Vltava.

215

- Meadow grass area in the summer with the grove of Platanus acerifolia planted into tree pits of five cubic metres.
▸ Pedestrian bridge.
▾ The overall roofscape.

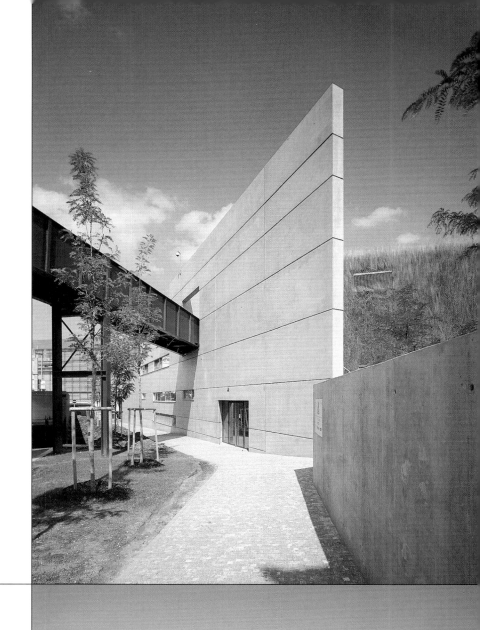

green wall are irrigated by a sub-surface Rainbird system and the trees are drip irrigated.

The development's mall provides north-south connections between Plzenska and Kartouská streets and there is also a 76-metre span steel footbridge at roof level over Kartouská linking the development to the park of Sacre Coeur and the suburbs above. This project is interesting in that green roof planting has been used to subdue the visual impact of a massive 60,000 square metre shopping mall development; at the same time it has improved connections within the city, while providing commercial retail development. The jury summed this up, "It's more than a roof garden, it's a vast landscape of no compromise".

Forum Romanum walkway

Programme Open spaces
and walkway through the
archaeological site of Forum
Romanum
Designer Michele Molé
with Maria Claudia Clemente
and Daniele Durante,
Nemesi Studio
Client City of Rome
Area not applicable
Design period 2001-2004
Implementation period
2001-2004
Cost € 800,000

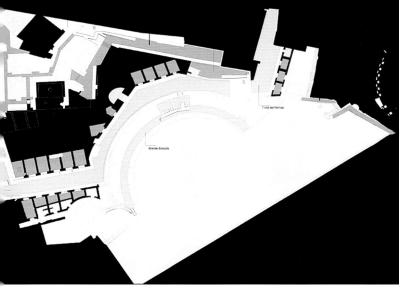

Trajan's Market in the distance and the new walkway making the connection.
The walkway passes along the walls of the Campo Carleo and creates a link between Suburra and the Via Biberatica.
Plan of the tabernae or semicircular layout of market shops which faced south here.

In the 1990s the Museo dei Fori Imperiali devised a major new way of interpreting the Roman Forum. This involved new archaeological digs, repaving and the provision of electrical security and fire prevention measures and creating an archaeological park. As part of this effort of reinterpretation Nemesi Studio were commissioned to provide a new connection, with disabled access, on the southern part of the Via Biberatica. This takes the form of a high-level walkway along the walls at the edge of the Augustan Forum and leads to the great semi circular Market of Trajan and to the shops of the tabernae. Trajan's Forum was built in 114 BC by Appollodorus of Damascus, and has six levels, so the task of providing easy access was not straightforward.

The Nemesi design involves two parts of the Forum, the tabernae on the Via Biberatica and a raised walkway on the Campo Carleo, which forms a link between the monuments of the Forum. The work on the Via Biberatica involved conserving the buildings and reinstating the original urban thoroughfare. The new walkway is a series of bridges of Corten steel which hardly touches the monuments; it is cantilevered, structurally independent, and it allows exploration.

The jury commented on this scheme as, "very well done where, as an archaeological site, an element of great simplicity" has been formed "which opens up the Forum and connects streets" so "allowing you to encounter all this protected structure to which previously you were denied access". The Forum was at the centre of Imperial Rome and indeed at the centre of the classical world and holds a unique place in Western civilization. Its treatment is a reflection of contemporary culture. The

▲ The tabernae or market shops and cellars on the Via Biberatica in Trajan's Market.
▼ Walkway in use.

Renaissance builders drew it, measured it and then used it as a quarry for rebuilding Rome, the nineteenth century excavated and in part destroyed late classical remains. Mussolini drove a major new road through it. This is an example of a far lighter, more respectful touch.

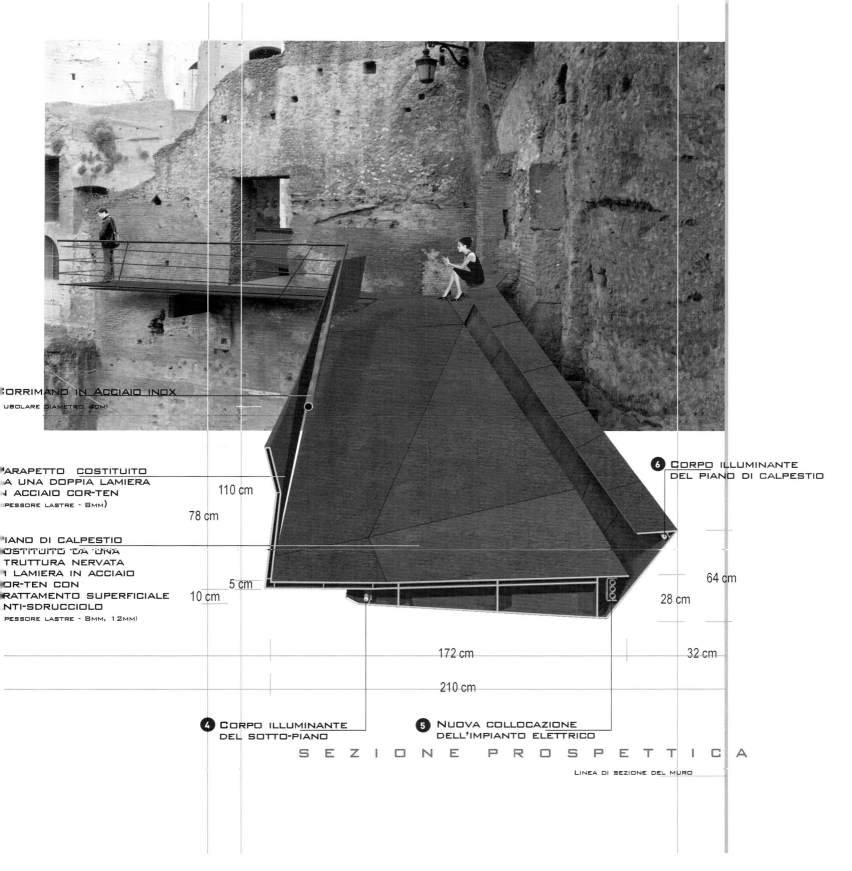

CORRIMANO IN ACCIAIO INOX
(TUBOLARE DIAMETRO 4CM)

PARAPETTO COSTITUITO
DA UNA DOPPIA LAMIERA
IN ACCIAIO COR-TEN
(SPESSORE LASTRE - 8MM)

110 cm

78 cm

PIANO DI CALPESTIO
COSTITUITO DA UNA
STRUTTURA NERVATA
A LAMIERA IN ACCIAIO
COR-TEN CON
TRATTAMENTO SUPERFICIALE
ANTI-SDRUCCIOLO
(SPESSORE LASTRE - 8MM, 12MM)

5 cm

10 cm

6 CORPO ILLUMINANTE
DEL PIANO DI CALPESTIO

64 cm

28 cm

172 cm

32 cm

210 cm

4 CORPO ILLUMINANTE
DEL SOTTO-PIANO

5 NUOVA COLLOCAZIONE
DELL'IMPIANTO ELETTRICO

S E Z I O N E   P R O S P E T T I C A

LINEA DI SEZIONE DEL MURO

◂ Sectional study.
1 4cm diameter stainless steel tubular handrail.
2 Parapet wal. of 8mm thick Corten steel sheet.
3 8mm and 12mm thick Corten steel sheet with antislip treatment.
4 Underlighting.
5 Electrical services.
6 Hidden lighting of the walkway floor.
◂ View from below shows minimal cantilevered structural support and the mirimum of
intervention.

221

Location Rotterdam (NL)

Nieuw-Terbregge Observatorium

Programme Public art for new
housing
Designer het Observatorium
Client Proper-Stok Woningen
bv, City of Rotterdam,
department for urban planning
Area 600 m^2
Design period 2000-2001
Implementation period 2001
Cost € 200,000

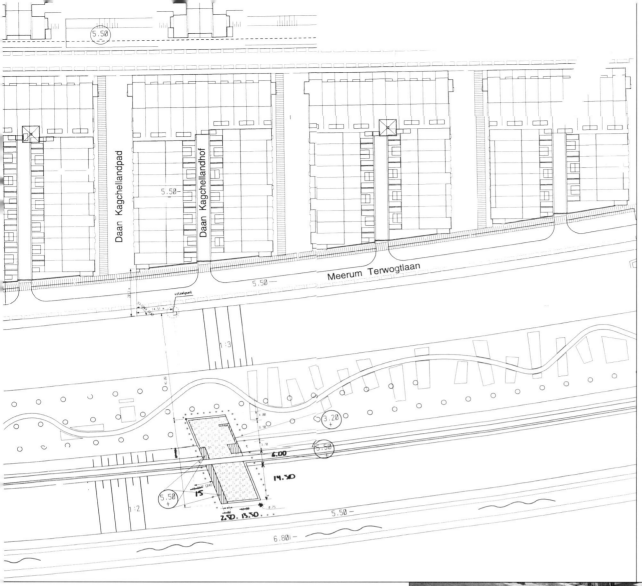

When a new housing estate is built in the Netherlands, the municipal council, planners and residents groups rack their brains over what form of public art should be erected. A place where the residents can relax and meet other people. Usually they come up with some form of sculpture or a specially designed park. Just such a special place has been created in the small Rotterdam urban extension of Nieuw-Terbregge. But not in the middle of the estate; neither is it a statue or pond. It is a sturdy pavilion on the embankment that runs between the estate and the A20 motorway.

The unusual idea of giving Nieuw-Terbregge a publicly accessible work of art came from Observatorium artists group (Geert van de Camp, Andre Dekker, Ruud Reutelingsperger). The developers, Proper-Stok Woningen bv, decided to support the initiative. A developer that is supportive and undertakes to cover the full cost is something special. And so were the results.

The artists chose the site on the embankment in order to confront the suburban world of peace and quiet with the motorway world of speed and noise. The Observatorium is a modern version of the traditional enclosed garden, the *hortus conclusus*, and consists of three elements: an exhibition pavilion, a paved garden and a viewpoint that overlooks both the estate and the motorway. The three elements refer to the fundamental elements of new housing estates in general: the house, the garden and the window for looking out on the street. The reference to the motorway lies in the use of materials. In fact, the whole complex is composed of old motorway materials. Vehicle safety fence elements have been used in the construction of the pavilion; asphalt has been reused in the garden and on the slopes of the embankment.

◂　The Observatorium.
▴　Construction drawing.
▴　The location of the complex near the A20.

▲ Re-use of asphalt and crash barriers.
◂ View of the Observatorium from the motorway.

The Observatorium is a folly designed to give the park an extra dimension, a welcome interruption in the walk through the park. It entices residents away from the park for a moment to visit the pavilion and perhaps linger a bit longer. Later, when they arrive at the viewpoint, the contrast with the seclusion of the pavilion is immense. They are suddenly confronted by the dynamic environment in which they live. On one side, the idyllic security of Nieuw-Terbregge, on the other, the fast-moving and risky outside world: the speeding cars (about 300,000 each day) and the Rotterdam skyline in the distance.

The Observatorium shows that landscape architecture and art are moving closer together. Landscape architects are making more frequent use of works of art in their designs; artists are increasingly demonstrating that they can produce well-crafted designs for landscape works. So far, the site has not been taken over by loitering gangs of youths and graffiti-sprayers. A monument to the first Rotterdam food-dropping sortie (Operation Manna) in May 1945 will be erected in 2006. The selection committee commends the reuse of motorway materials. The artists could not have made a better link with the A20 in this masculine design.

↥ View from the pavilion.
↤ The viewpoint.

Salou Seafront promenade

Programme Public use of
a natural coastline
Designer Jordi Belmunt,
Xavier Andreu
In collaboration with
Olga Alonso, Agata Buscemi
Client GP Resort Port Aventura
Area 2.9 ha
Design period 2003–2004
Implementation period 2004
Cost € 2,500,000

The design for the promenade of P.atja Llarga.
The green nature of the coast forms a haven between the busy Spanish seaside resorts.

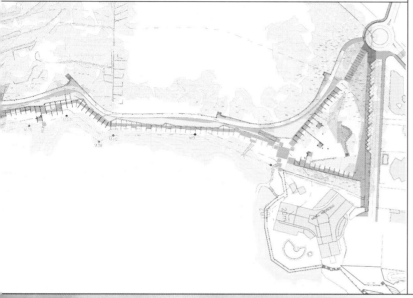

Coasts are intriguing places. Where land and water meet, and where mass tourism has not yet taken over, this natural gradient creates virgin landscapes. Between the Spanish coastal resort of Salou and a spit of land to the west lies the strip of coast known as Platja Llarga. This stretch of coastline is a completely different world from the crowded boulevard in Salou, with its hotels, restaurants, beach bars and scantily clad bathers. Pine trees, Evergreen Pistache, Mediterranean Fan Palm and agaves characterise the dominant vegetation in the landscape, next to the wide sweep of sea, sand and rocks.

Resort Port Aventura, a large bungalow park in Salou, would dearly like to open up this rough, imposing landscape for the holidaymakers in its parks. Platja Llarga offers adventure, attractive walks and peace and quiet, in contrast to the predictability of the promenade in Salou.

The design by Jordi Bellmunt and Xavier Andreu arranges public use of the coastline like a promenade, while reinforcing the natural landscape. The designers talk of a plan that emerged in dialogue with the landscape. The sharp division between sea and land has been accentuated and the vegetation has been brought back to the dune edge. A low white wall, which also serves as a bench, divides the beach from the dunes and also

serves as the promenade. Openings have been made at regular intervals along the megabank. This linear element defines in the clearest possible way what is appropriate where and what is not. You may fly a kite on the beach, but not on the promenade; you can lay out your towel on the beach, but not on the promenade. The promenade is paved with concrete slabs on a bed of sand, each of which has been air treated to obtain a slightly uneven surface. In the evening, linear lighting elements pick out the clear straight line of the promenade and metres-long bench bisecting the landscape. It creates a visual link between the urban landscape of Sa ou and the wooded landscape of Platja Llarga, as well as the land and the sea.

The slopes in the woods have been replanted with traditional dune plants such as tamarisk, narcissus and germander. Old walls that protect the land from the sea where there is no beach have been restored with local rocks. Familiar regional scents from the lavender, agave, Spanish broom, thyme, ivy and Evergreen Pistache hang in the air. The promenade is easily accessible along its full length, with concrete steps between the upper and lower parts. Wheelchair access is available, including viewpoints.

The design looks beyond the coastal strip and brings in the relevant landward areas. The selection committee stresses the need to manage the processes of erosion both by natural forces and from recreational pressure. The committee was impressed by the graceful and relaxed feel to the plan: the materials used rest quietly in the landscape, as if they have always been there.

- Impression of the natural coastal landscape and the promenade from the sea.
- Points of light streamline the promenade in the evening.
- Use of different kinds of materials.
- The vegetation has been brought back to the dune edge.

▸ ▲ A low white wall divides the beach from the dunes.
▲ Cross sections (western and eastern part).
▾ Acces to the terraces of the western part of the promenade.

Cendon di Silea riverside

Programme A series of urban open spaces in the old centre of Cendon di Silea
Designer Adriano Maragon and Michela De Poli, made associati
Client municipality of Silea
Area 8,000 m^2
Design period 2002-2004
Implementation period 2004
Cost € 1,200,000

◄▲ The riverside which once was inaccessible now becomes accessible to all.
◄ A design of austere simplicity made more so in winter when the quayside floods.
▲ "Before" view: A village set in fields beside the River Fiume Sile but no longer actively used. The geometry of the field patterns is reflected in the design.
   (Photos: Adriano Maragon and Corrado Piccoli)

The old centre of the town of Cendon di Silea is spread along the River Sile and faces across the river to agricultural fields beyond. The river was formerly the source of power for the mills and the main means of communication but the area has now become run down, buildings have fallen out of use and access to the river has been difficult. These problems led to a competition in 1998 to develop the potential of the riverside.

Made Associati have now begun a series of projects which will reveal the riverside. Their design has two main spatial characteristics taken from the town and the countryside: the opportunity for creating spaces by opening up the land around the present buildings and reflecting the field plot patterns across the river. In places, the town frontage to the river was not accessible: some areas, such as the church sacristy, a bar and some gardens, were enclosed and fenced while the frontage to the fields was fragmented with buildings backing onto the river and some yards, empty areas and uncultivated field plots.

The design is in a series of phases. The first involves the establishment of a series of green structures such as alleys of trees enclosing the car park, and the replacement of fences by mixed agriculturally-derived hedges. The next stage involved the creation of public spaces giving access to the river: a new space facing the river next to an existing bar, a church square, forming part of a major public square, and a cycle park and piazza next to an information centre. These are connected by a renewed quayside, set close to the level of the river just 50 centimetres above the water. A network of paths connects these spaces. There are

231

▲ | ▾ New gardens have been created near the church.
▲ A simple range of materials has been used.

also a series of counterpoints such as the campanile of the church, which relates to a poplar grove across the river. These new spaces and paths have been constructed in a simple range of materials using Corten steel, timber and stone. The pattern of the historical context of town and countryside has been reflected in the plan. The jury thought this, "a very quiet and gentle scheme, as Italy tends to use its rivers as dumps... so this is a significant example of using a river well, it fits the scale of the town and spatially is beautiful".

R verside boardwalks simply detailed.

Norrlands hospital gardens

Programme Design of a
hospital garden, consisting
of two parts on either side
of a glass connecting passage.
Designer GORA art &
landscape
Client Västerbotten County
Area 4,746 m^2
Design period 2001
Implementation period
2001-2002
Cost € 100,000

▲ Nature up to the wall. The lush meadow is dotted with b rch, pine and alder and colourful sculptures. (Photos: Jan Lindmark)

▼ The technical plan. The circles represent the trees planted, the rectangles the sculptures.

The blood-testing department of the university hospital in the northern Swedish city of Umeå moved to brand-new premises several years ago. This building was connected to the old part of the hospital by a glass passageway. Two half-open inner gardens came into being on either side of the passageway. The hospital management had traditional gardens with lawns and flower beds designed for the two areas and asked Monika Gora of GORA art & landscape to make a statue for the garden. In the end, Gora did not make the statue but made a completely new design for the two outside spaces.

According to the landscape architect and artist, the two spaces must be arranged in such a way that they form a sturdy and natural buffer between the very stony surroundings of the hospital buildings and the glass passage. The outer and inner spaces of the glass connecting hall in particular are the equivalent of each other in her design "Common Ground".

The two gardens have been planted with grasses and colourful, indigenous flowers to be like lush meadows. In these meadows Gora set trees and sculptures which remind most of a heart or a flower. These two basic elements are spread over the two gardens as well as the glass corridor. Visitors will think that the elements have been placed randomly. In reality the trees and the sculptures follow the modelling of the ground. This creates the image of a green slope on which the trees and sculptures seem to glide like skiers from one garden to the other through the glass passage. The connection between interior and exterior is reinforced by extending the limestone tile floor to the outer patios, which

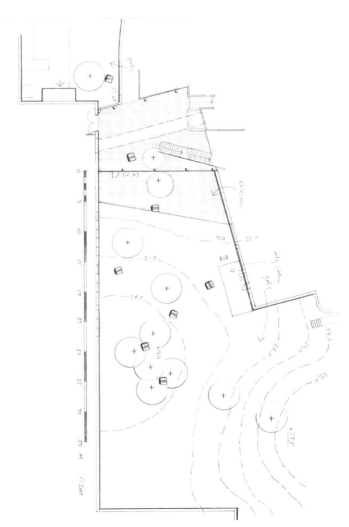

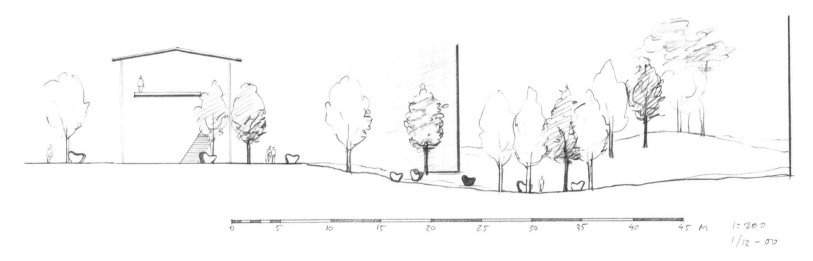

- ▲ The cross section shows how the trees and sculptures seem to flow from one garden through the glass passage to the other garden.
- ◄ The sculptures are often used as sofa. Inside the exotic tree species Podocarpus graciliosa.
- ▼ The cement tiles of the patio are a visual link with the limestone floor inside.

The sculptures seem to glide like skiers from one garden to the other through the glass passage. The sakes show were the trees will be planted.
Special illumination in the evening.

has been carried out in limestone-look concrete tiles because limestone is not hardy enough for outside use.

Gora uses subtle techniques to reflect the difference between outside and inside. In the glass corridor, there is an exotic tree species of conifer (*Podocarpus graciliosa*), whilst outside northern Swedish species like birch, pine and alder have been planted. The colours of the sculptures refer to the blood tests that take place in the surrounding buildings. They are in colours from the same pigment (magenta) but in different concentrations from deep purple to light pink. Magenta is also the colour of a flower that is common locally: the rosebay willow-herb (*Epilobium angustifolium*). One of the sculptures is black.

This is the original, made of granite. The others are all replicas, made of polyester. The sculptures are primarily used by visitors and staff as a place to sit, because of their sofa-like shape. There are lamps in the sculptures. This gives a special kind of illumination, especially in the winter when it is already dark at three in the afternoon.

The design is spectacular in its simplicity. According to the jury Gora follows a well-chosen concept: she allows nature to come up to the walls of the building without making an issue of it. The sculptures are attractive to look at and functional at the same time. The illumination of the elements is essential in the eyes of the jury members in a region where it is dark for much of the year.

Grounds in the Park Village office complex

Programme Design of a plaza and rooftop gardens for a newly built office complex
Designer Burger Landschaftsarchitekten
In collaboration with MVRDV, Lauber architekten, BGSP+K (architecture)
Client Merkur GmbH & Co, Objekt Unterföhring KG
Area 1.6 ha
Design period 1999-2001
Implementation period 2001-2003
Cost € 1,700,000

▸ | ⇥ The landscape extends on two levels: the ground and the rooftops. By pushing a single homogeneous stone plaza under the free-standing independent office buildings the complex is joined to an overall whole, perceptible when walking through it or looking down from the windows.

◄ Water channels drain the area
   and form a frame around each
   building.
- Axonometric view of the office
   complex.

Halfway between downtown and the airport is one of Munich's major urban development areas for the service industry: Unterföhring. In the last few years, many insurance and media companies have settled here on land made available for new construction. Right opposite Swiss Re's well-known new building surrounded by a wisteria-and-vine treillage that people can walk around on (architects: Bothe Richter Teherani, Hamburg), an investor is now developing the opposite of the introverted office complex of the reinsurance company. Park Village is a small open "village" consisting of 19 different rectangular parallelipedal buildings. They are to provide an urban neighbourhood for a large number of office tenants, and some day they might develop into the heart of Unterföhring. The master plan of MVRDV consists of two construction phases. The first phase is completed with five buildings by the Rotterdam architects and four buildings by Munich's lauber architects. With varying heights, facades, materials and colours, they clearly create the desired heterogeneity of the "village". The second phase has not started yet.

The landscape architect Susanne Burger had the task of giving this variety some uniformity in terms of urban space. She took the theme of variety in unity in that she organized the open spaces on two levels, as proposed by the master plan. She pushed a single homogeneous stone plaza under the freestanding parallelipeds. This joins the complex into an overall whole, perceptible when walking through it or looking down from the windows. She topped the roofs with lively colourful gardens. This emphasizes the independence of each building, perceptible when looking from the upper storeys or the rooftop terraces across the rising and falling landscape of rooftops at varying heights.

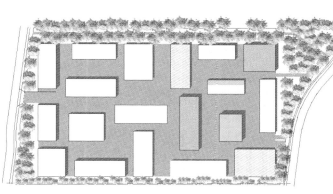

The strictly orthogonal ground plan is contrasted by the polygonal structure of the natural stone slabs which feature grass joints in varying widths.

Burger Landschaftsarchitecten's design contrasts the strictly orthogonal "urban ground plan" with paving made of polygonal natural stone slabs and grass joints in various widths. Thus the man-made buildings seem to rise up from natural ground marked by the irregular shapes, the rough texture of the 14-centimetre-thick slabs of Wachenzell dolomite, and the punches of grass sprouting cheekily from the joints. The planners had two guiding principles in their design. On the one hand, they put narrow joints where the pedestrian flow goes from building to building and where the deliveries and fire lanes are and wider joints in the rest of the area, which together create a vivid green network. On the other, they drain the area by means of water channels, each forming a frame around a building at a distance of two to four metres. More design was not necessary. The plaza was kept free of benches and other street furniture. The lighting comes from three tall floodlights near where the central café puts out its tables and chairs in the summer; elsewhere the light from the offices shines into the outdoor space after dark. This approach, tying the buildings together into one unit using minimal means, was what particularly convinced the jury. The jury expressly commended the urban "platter" consisting of no more than stones and joints.

The landscape architects designed the roof gardens, most of which are not accessible, according to themes. They created extensively planted roofs, two with a yellow carpet of sedum, one with a garden of blue grasses, one with a reddish heather cover, one with a violet field of lavender, one with an orange-and-blue field of flowers, one with a field of broom, another with a blue-and-yellow meadow of wild flowers. The last – featuring the bar of the café – is paved with polygonal slabs and planted with Irish moss.

◂ ▴ The polygonal stone slabs accompany the walkways at the northern edge of Park Village.
▴ | ▾ A reddish carpet of heather (Calluna vulgaris in varieties, Erica carnea in varieties) covers one of the rooftops, and fancy forms of lavender (Lavandula angustifolia) form a violet field on another.

Acoustic barrier at Leidsche Rijn

Programme Design and
construction plan for an
acoustic barrier
Designer ONL
Client Projectbureau
Leidsche Rijn, Hessing bv
Area 8,800 m^2
Design period 2002–2005
Implementation period 2005
Cost € 6,600,000 (wall),
€ 5,000,000 (cockpit)

The limits of outward urban expansion around cities are often defined by physical boundaries, such as motorways. Barriers have been erected throughout the Netherlands to cushion housing estates from traffic noise. For many years little attention was paid to the appearance of these elements, which line the busiest traffic arteries in the country. These noise barriers were seen foremost as functional objects. Concrete walls or earth embankments planted with trees worked perfectly well. This lack of interest in the aesthetics of noise barriers, or "acoustic barriers" in modern parlance, is actually rather strange. After all, thousands of car travellers look out onto a panorama of noise barriers every day. For years the visual experience of the motorist has been undervalued. But environmental psychological research has shown that people travelling on motorways are highly aware of the passing landscape. Now the numbers of projects that focus on clothing infrastructure landscapes are rising.

Automotive City by ONL, the multidisciplinary design office of Kas Oosterhuis and Ilona Lénárd, is one such example. Along the A2 where it passes the massive new Leidsche Rijn extension of Utrecht, ONL have designed a one-and-a-half kilometre acoustic barrier. The Leidsche Rijn project office were convinced that the design of this noise barrier had to be special. The most famous urban extension in the Netherlands needed an icon, like the Erasmus Bridge for the Kop van Zuid in Rotterdam. The challenge facing ONL was to design the barrier as an icon that would be seen by everyone.

The design for the structure is based on the fact that motorists travelling at 120 kilometres per hour pass the barrier in forty seconds. The grid-like

‹   Animation of the acoustic barrier.
↟   The barrier with the De Wetering-Noord Industrial Estate behind it.
▲   3D model for the acoustic barrier.

interplay of steel lines that make up the barrier has been stretched by a factor 10, in what is called "elastic architecture". The lines seem to have no beginning or end. The structure seemingly moves with the eyes of the motorist to prevent any startling visual changes, even though the thirteen-metre-high barrier is motionless.

The slim body of the barrier is interrupted half way along by a bulge. This "Cockpit" has been included in the barrier for Hessing, dealers in luxury cars, as a showroom for Bentley and Rolls Royce. In the evening LED lighting elements pinpoint both ends of the wall. The rounded ends contain electronic message signs with information for the companies in the De Wetering-Noord business estate behind the barrier.

Even though Automotive city is primarily a structural and architectural element, it has a major impact on the landscape – in a positive way. The selection committee believes that ONL have been successful in creating a relatively cheap and attractive noise barrier which meets several goals at the same time. It is an asset for the motorway landscape travelled by many people every day. There was less appreciation, though, for the inclusion of a car dealership in the Cockpit element. In the opinion of the selection committee the construction of an acoustic barrier is a direct consequence of the high traffic volumes, so it is a pity that one of its uses is to promote car sales.

- The steel lines have no beginning and no end.
- The structure seems to move with the motorist.

Weiach churchyard

Programme Extension of
an existing churchyard
Designer Kuhn Truninger
Landschaftsarchitekten
Client municipality of Weiach
Area 1,700 m^2
Design period 2001-2003
Implementation period
2003-2004
Cost € 375,000

◄ Nord

◄ The new graveyard is set in the middle of the village with the new extension to the east. A gravel path leads from the church to the graveyard extension through the parsonage courtyard to the south.

↟ Churchyard entrance with its Pawlonia tree and fountain.

▴ An artists impression of the churchyard.
(Photos: Ralph Feiner)

Weiach is a small village of less than a thousand people in the northern part of the Canton of Zurich near the River Rhine. This project involved an extension of the old churchyard. The existing site layout dates from the early 18th century and is a grouping of church, parsonage, and old stone walled churchyard, originally fortified because of religious wars of the time. The church and its churchyards, old and new, are set in the middle of the small, rural village with views to orchards. The new extension is very much of the present, a totally new enclosure to the east of the church.

The new graveyard is enclosed by a two metre high screen of upright l larch boards spaced so as to form a semi permeable barrier, through which you can just see through, catching glimpses from the outside, when at some angles to the fence. This screen recalls the fences around local nurseries and also reminds us of the earlier timber fences around the churchyard. At night this screen is lit, which makes it more impressive and solemn, its verticality is emphasized, like a series of lit tributes, such as stele or ancient grave markers which denote the boundaries and further emphasize the enclosure of the space. The new cemetery allows several forms of burial: classic burial, burial in urns, communal grave or a meadow grave. The whole burial ground is punctuated by fine polished grey concrete slabs marked by inset bronze crosses which correspond to the geometry of the old cemetery and so establish a relationship between old and new.

▲ The present day view with the new extension to the graveyard to the right of the church.
◄ The entrance fountain of polished concrete.
▼ A simple vertical larch fence provides the enclosure.

Pawlonia trees mark a water feature of polished concrete by the entrance which provides a prelude to the controlled simplicity beyond. The jury saw this scheme as having "great simplicity, very poetic, based on tradition but also very contemporary; it relates and reverberates with the old churchyard and the spatial relationship is beautiful." In short, this design has "a clear concept". The ensemble is rigorously, almost austerely, simple, vigorously of its time yet respectful of its surroundings: it is simple and appropriate for a small community and a modest way of life.

- The historic ensemble of church, village and fields which still exists.
- The superbly finished concrete pavig slap with inset bronze crosses orientated to align with the geometry of the old churchyard.
- The new enclosure.
- At night the vertical timber fence is lit to form a series of stelae.

Location Weingarten (D)

Weingarten city garden

Programme Public park with café, concert stage, central bus stop, and underground car park
Designer Lohrer.Hochrein Landschaftsarchitekten BDLA and Rolf Bürhaus (architecture)
Client City of Weingarten
Area 1.7 ha
Design period 2000-2001
Implementation period 2002-2004
Cost € 800,000 (only park)

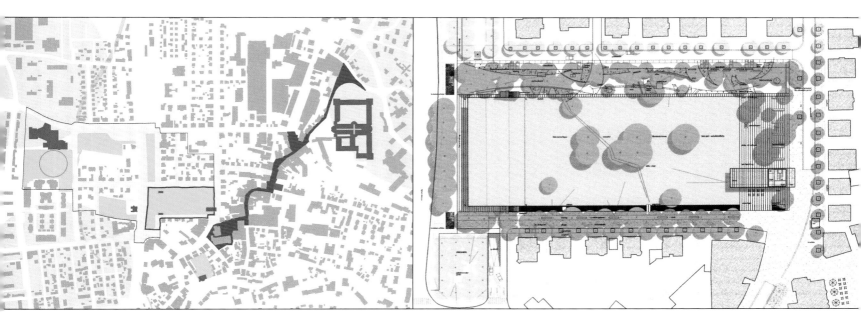

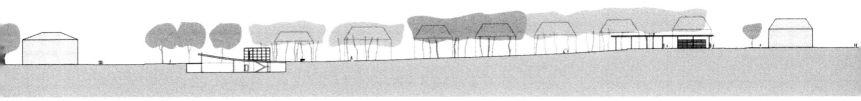

A relic of the 19th century, rebuilt several times, overgrown in the course of time, half of it used as a car park, plagued by noise from the adjacent four-lane federal motorway – even the playground equipment set up in the shade of its trees a few years ago could not obscure the fact that Weingarten's city park was in a miserable state. Change never came until the design competition held by the municipal administration in 1999. The park was to be brought back into the centre of town – into the network of interconnected routes running from the historical basilica and the pedestrian precinct in the east to the cultural forum, the schools, the recreational facilities and several green areas in the west, and from the

‹ ⮝ Slightly sloping down from the urban terrace of the café, the park is re-establishing the link between the pedestrian precinct of the historical centre in the east to the cultural forum and several green areas in the west.

⮝ Ground plan.

⮝ The lawn carpet angles upwards to cover a parking garage and to protect the park from traffic noise, as shown in the section.

‹ View of the playing area.

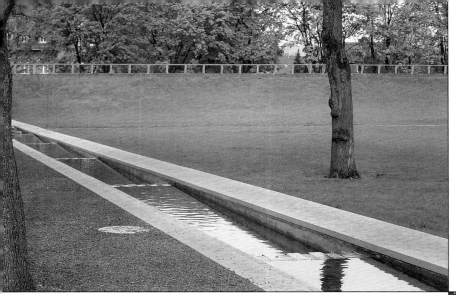

‹ | ▾ From a water table by the café, a watercourse leads along the south edge of the park.

residential neighbourhoods in the north to those in the south. With their design for a spacious "green plaza", the landscape architects Axel Lohrer and Ursula Hochrein of Waldkraiburg won over the competition jury. They proposed building an urban terrace at the upper end of the park, with outdoor seating for a café, an open-air concert stage and a central bus stop. From the terrace, they unrolled a velvety lawn carpet under the massive trees. It angles upwards towards the motorway, forming a slope that protects the park from traffic noise, and houses a naturally lit underground parking garage. The landscape architects envisaged the lawn as free and open, contrasting with the terrace, teeming with restless activity, rising up out of the city centre over the lush greenery. Only the trees and their shifting shadows accent the broad surface; freestanding seating and deck chairs invite users to relax and get together. Here everyone can take a deep breath.

Lohrer and Hochrein flank the northern side of the lawn carpet with a playground in a clearing under the existing trees. Here toddlers can find sand and water to play with, bigger children swings and climbing frames, young people ping-pong and a floor chessboard, and the accompanying adults sunny or shady places to sit. On the south side, the landscape architects installed a watercourse that bubbles down playfully from a water table by the café, then forms a broad channel bordering the lawn carpet and finally tumbles down into the depths of the underground garage in a waterfall by the stairwell tower. In addition, the planners closed off the park towards the road with two fountain curtains on either side of the sloping lawn. The sheets of water cover up the sight and sound of the motor vehicles. The jury compared the park with Sven Ingvar Andersson's Museumplein in Amsterdam, where one edge also bends upward to form a slope. They preferred Weingarten's lawn carpet, however, because it slopes much more generously – namely in its full width. The jury allowed itself to be carried away by the simplicity of the design and its beautiful details: "A mature and powerful project, whose authors know what they want."

- The park extends as a green plaza from the urban terrace of the café.
- From the terrace, the landscape architects unrolled a velvety lawn carpet under the old trees and integrated sculptures.
- Fountains on the side of the sloping lawn close the park off toward the road.

Imprint

Edited by
Landscape Architecture Europe Foundation,
Schip van Blaauw, Generaal Foulkesweg 72, BW 6703 Wageningen,
The Netherlands
www.landscapearchitectureeurope.com

Board of the Foundation
Meto Vroom (chairman)
Professor emeritus for landscape architecture at Wageningen University
Annalisa Maniglio Calcagno
*Professor of landscape architecture at the School of Architecture, University
of Genova*
Isabel Figueras Ponsa
*Landscape architect and lecturer at the ETSAB School of Architecture,
Polytechnic University Barcelona*
Joseph de Gryse
Landscape architect and former president of EFLA Brussels
Robert Holden
Professor of landscape architecture at Greenwich University, London

Selection jury
Michael van Gessel (chairman)
Landscape architect, Amsterdam
Stig L. Andersson
Architect, founding director of SLA Landscape Architects, Copenhagen
Henri Bava
*Partner of the Agence Ter landscape architecture practice and professor at
Karlsruhe University, Karlsruhe*
Robert Camlin
Director, Camlin Lonsdale Landscape Architects, Wales
Maria Goula
*Landscape architect and lecturer at the ETSAB Architecture School,
Barcelona*

Secretariat and production
Harry Harsema
Landscape architect and publisher, Wageningen
Mark Hendriks
Spatial planner and journalist, Wageningen
Anne Marie Roetgerink
Secretariat

Editorial board
Lisa Diedrich (chief editor)
Architect and landscape architecture critic, Munich
Robert Holden
*Professor of landscape architecture and lecturer at Greenwich University,
London*
Eric Luiten
Landscape architect and critic, Utrecht

Essays
Lisa Diedrich
Malene Hauxner
Karin Helms
Robert Holden
Gertjan Jobse
Hansjörg Küster
Lionella Scazzosi

Project texts
Lisa Diedrich
Mark Hendriks
Robert Holden
Eric Luiten

Translation into English
Marion Frandsen (essay Hauxner)
Catrin Gersdorf (essay Küster)
Derek Middleton (project texts)
Almuth Seebohm (essays Diedrich und Helms, project texts)

Text editing
Maris van der Laak
Nick Parrott

Design, lithography and image processing
Daphne de Bruijn and Harry Harsema, Grafisch Atelier Wageningen
Hans Dijkstra, Wim van Hof and Harry van Oosterhout, bvBeeld
Wageningen

Illustrations
All illustrations by the autors and the selected offices, unless noted

Printing
Ludwig Auer, Donauwörth, Germany
Printed on acid-free paper produced from chlorine-free pulp. TCF ∞

European Foundation for Landscape Architecture

Stimuleringsfonds
voor Architectuur

the Netherlands
Architecture Fund

Landscape Architecture Europe is an initiative of the Landscape
Architecture Europe Foundation (LAE) and the European Foundation for
Landscape Architecture (EFLA).
The publication was made possible by the provision of subsidy from the
Netherlands Architecture Fund and the HGIS Culture Fund of the
Ministries of Foreign Affairs, and of Education, Culture and Science

A CIP catalogue record for this book is available from the Library of
Congress, Washington D.C., USA

Bibliographic information published by Die Deutsche Bibliothek.
Die Deutsche Bibliothek lists this publication in the Deutsche
Nationalbibliografie; detailed bibliographic data is available in the
internet at http://dnb.ddb.de.

This book is also available in a German language edition
ISBN 3-7643-7507-8).

© 2006 Birkhäuser –Publishers for Architecture,
P. O. Box 133, CH-4010 Basel, Switzerland
Part of Springer Science + Business Media

ISBN-10: 3-7243-7508-6
ISBN-13: 978-3-7643-7508-9

9 8 7 6 5 4 3 2 1
www.birkhauser.ch